The Unlimited Universe Awaits

Enter a realm in which time and space have no meaning; a world where thought is action, and simple desire can take you anywhere you want to go—enter the astral domain.

Astral Projection for Beginners provides step-by-step instructions for six different methods of astral projection: general transfer of consciousness, meditating toward astral separation, guided meditation, using symbolic gateways, projecting through the chakras, and stepping out of your dreams. If you've always been curious about astral travel but were worried about its safety, this book will reassure you.

Learn how the seven chakras serve as portals between our physical selves and the astral world, and about their role in remote healing. Gain spiritual understanding and growth by viewing your Akashic Records, the etheric record of all past and future events, thoughts, and actions for each living soul from the time of its creation. Travel to different times and dimensions to visit the realm of faeries, view past lives, or reunite with departed loved ones.

The unlimited universe is both inside and outside of yourself. It only awaits you to challenge and explore the boundaries of the ordinary.

About the Author

Edain McCoy received her first set of divination cards as a teenager. She began reading tarot for others in her midtwenties, and by her thirties was experimenting successfully with the challenges of creating her own spreads. An alumnus of the University of Texas with a bachelor of arts in history, she is affiliated with several professional writer's organizations and is listed in the reference guides *Contemporary Authors* and *Who's Who in America*. Articles by her have appeared in *FATE, Circle, Enlightenments,* and similar periodicals. Edain also worked for ten years as a stockbroker with several large investment firms. This former woodwind player for the Lynchburg Symphony claims both the infamous feuding McCoy family of Kentucky and Sir Roger Williams, the seventeenth-century religious dissenter, as branches on her diverse family tree.

To Write to the Author

If you wish to contact the author or would like more information about this book, please write to the author in care of Llewellyn Worldwide and we will forward your request. Both the author and the publisher appreciate hearing from you and learning of your enjoyment of this book and how it has helped you. Llewellyn Worldwide cannot guarantee that every letter written to the author can be answered, but all will be forwarded. Please write to:

Edain McCoy
c/o Llewellyn Worldwide
2143 Wooddale Drive, Dept. 978-1-56718-625-3
Woodbury, MN 55125-2989 U.S.A.

Please enclose a self-addressed, stamped envelope for reply, or $1.00 to cover costs. If outside the U.S.A., enclose international postal reply coupon.

ASTRAL
PROJECTION
for BEGINNERS

Learn Several Techniques to Gain
a Broad Awareness of Other Realms
of Existence

Edain McCoy

Llewellyn Publications
Woodbury, Minnesota

FIRST EDITION
Tenth Printing, 2009

Cover design by Adrienne Zimiga
Interior design and editing by Kjersti Monson
Interior illustrations by Bill Cannon

Library of Congress Cataloguing-in-Publication Data
    McCoy, Edain, 1957–
        Astral projection for beginners : learn several techniques
    to gain a broad awareness of other realms of existence / Edain
    McCoy. — 1st ed.
            p. cm.
        Includes bibliographical references and index.
        ISBN 13: 978-1-56718-625-3
        ISBN 10: 1-56718-625-4
        1. Astral projection.   I. Title.
    BF1389.A7M36   1999   98–51538
    133.9'5—dc21   CIP

Llewellyn Publications
A Division of Llewellyn Worldwide, Ltd.
2143 Wooddale Drive, Dept. 978-1-56718-625-3
Woodbury, MN 55125-2989
www.llewellyn.com
Llewellyn is a registered trademark of Llewellyn Worldwide, Ltd.
Printed in the United States of America

Other Books by Edain McCoy

Witta: An Irish Pagan Tradition

A Witch's Guide to Faery Folk

Sabbats

How to Do Automatic Writing

Celtic Myth and Magick

Magick & Rituals of the Moon (formerly titled *Lady of the Night*)

Entering the Summerland

Mountain Magick

The Witch's Coven

Making Magick

Celtic Women's Spirituality

Bewitchments

Enchantments

Ostara

Spellworking or Covens

Advanced Witchcraft

If You Want to Be a Witch

Sabbats

Past-Life & Karmic Tarot

Contents

Introduction

Welcome to a world in which time and space have no meaning and no influence. This is the world known as the astral plane, an ethereal realm that is often perceived as being parallel to and interpenetrating our own physical world, but which remains unseen by the eyes of our normal consciousness.

In keeping with the old occult adage, "As above, so below; as within, so without," the astral plane exists both within and outside of ourselves. This adage also reminds us that we have the power to create our worlds, meaning that what we find inside ourselves (in the non-physical world of the mind) is reflected by the conditions outside of ourselves (in the physical world). Therefore, what is allowed to affect us from outside of ourselves eventually manifests within. We can travel to or help to create any of those worlds—inner or outer—through astral projection.

Astral projection is the art of sending forth the consciousness at will to other places, other worlds, or other times, and then bringing it back with full knowledge of what has been experienced. This projected consciousness is sometimes referred to as the *astral body,* hence the term *astral projection.*

Examining the many synonyms that we have for astral projection tells us a lot about the people who coined those terms as well as those who still use them. The synonyms include: mental projection, mind travel, soul travel, mind journey, traveling in the spirit vision, traveling in the emotional body, remote viewing, lucid dreaming, and bi-location.

With all of these terms being bandied about, it's no wonder that there is an argument among practitioners of the art as to just what the astral body is comprised of. Also in dispute is what part of us it is (if any) that actually ventures forth on these astral journeys.

Some go so far as to say that it is a part of the soul that willingly parts from its physical home to travel forth, remaining attached to the host body by only a thin silver cord, which, if severed, would cause the projector's death. These proponents often refer to astral projection as an OBE, an acronym for *out-of-body experience*.

Others say that it is only the astral self who leaves. They define astral self as an emotional layer of our non-physical selves—an ethereal body that tightly surrounds us like a second aura and acts as a conduit between the consciousness, the higher self, and the outside world. These proponents view the astral plane as a definite geographical point outside of ourselves.

Still others say that only the consciousness journeys forth, suggesting that a part of our mind reaches out from the body by actually going deep within itself. They often refer to the astral realm as the *inner planes*, and accept themselves as a mirror of the macrocosm—a reflection of the entire universe.

A large part of our confusion over what astral projection is and what it is supposed to feel like can also be blamed on semantics, since words are often insufficient to describe the phenomenon of projection. We find ourselves repeatedly using phrases like *out, out-of-body, going out, flying*, etc., when discussing the experience because this is simply what it feels like. Even those who feel that you really go nowhere other than deep inside yourself have no choice but to use this kind of language to describe and teach the process. No other words are adequate.

As a result of imprecise language, we are led to the very misconceptions we presumably hope to dispel. This has caused beginners to form false preconceptions about what defines successful astral projection. Many occult books, both fiction and non-fiction, depict astral projection as something that it simply is not. No one would argue that astral projection does not have its spectacular moments, but most often the feelings it creates are not as stunning as we are led to believe they should be. To compound the problem, it can feel different each time you project, depending on the astral situation in which you find yourself.

The truth is, you almost always retain an awareness of your physical body while you are astral projecting, rather than being completely divorced from your physical self. Too many people get frustrated and feel that they have failed because they are not lost in a world where the physical is completely forgotten. While this may occasionally happen, you will usually just find yourself in a state of expanded awareness where both worlds are equally real. In other words, you will be *wholly* conscious, perhaps more so than at any other time in your life. You will be able to access thoughts, memories, and impressions from all levels of your brain, mind, and self. Furthermore, in your projected state, you will choose to focus the bulk of your mental energy on the events and experiences of the astral world rather than on those of the physical.

Any time that you are wholly involved in a time or place removed from your physical body, or are simultaneously aware of both your physical self and a self that seems somehow distanced from your body, you are astral projecting. Intense daydreaming is a type of astral projection. Think about all those times you've been lost in deep thought—times when the inner world became so real that you temporarily forgot the physical one. Chances are, someone may have come along and waved a hand in front of your face to break your trance and asked, "Where were you?" Notice again the use of language referring to being outside of yourself. Also, think about a time when you have experienced intense physical or emotional pain. Do you recall moving though those events as if you were not wholly there, that somehow you were distanced from your physical body and were watching it go through the motions of living while the real you was somewhere else? These are both astral projection experiences, though many people never recognize them as such.

What people refer to as the *astral plane* encompasses the entire physical and non-physical universe. Even the coherent thoughts of humanity live on the astral plane in what we call *thoughtforms,* or semi-solid projections of consciousness that have been built up over the years by living beings who need those daydream worlds to balance what is lacking in their physical ones. Who is to say which one is more real than the other?

The essence of the astral plane can be summed up in the old occult adage, "Thought is action on the astral plane." The simple act of will or coherent desire should take you anywhere you want to go, propel you into any situation you wish to find yourself, or call to you almost any being in existence. This is one of the reasons why it will be very important for you to go into the experience in a relaxed state and with a positive outlook. Chapters 3 and 4 will go into this in detail. Any feelings and energies that you take into the astral plane will be magnified and acted upon either by you or by other beings with whom you come into contact, and negative emotions or intentions will quickly rebound on you.

As I have learned from questions and letters that I have received over the years, many people get frustrated by what they perceive as their failed efforts to astral project. The common thread I find behind these lamentations is that most of these seekers have put serious effort into their practice and, in most cases, are succeeding without being aware they are succeeding. Again, we can thank popular misconceptions for leading these valiant astral travelers astray.

Astral projection is no more difficult to accomplish than any other skill that takes practice in order to become proficient. It actually takes a good deal less time than mastering many other skills. You can safely bet that a concert pianist has spent a lot more time practicing than you will have to invest in astral projection. The trick is in understanding the process, finding the method that works best for you, and then persisting until you succeed on a regular basis.

Astral projection is more than just an occult art. It's magic. Don't let this word scare you. Magic at its most basic is nothing more than transformation, especially self-transformation. When you seek spiritual knowledge, as you will in learning and using astral projection, you will find yourself changed. This is the art of making magic, and it's both positive and natural.

Once you master the art of astral projection, the universe is yours to explore. You can travel through time, view past lives, explore other worlds or planets, heal others, engage in astral sex with loving spirit partners, build sturdy psychic self-defense barriers, visit the home of the elements, and create personal rituals that are more potent than any you can enact on the physical plane.

You can also view what are known as the Akashic Records, compendiums of all knowledge about your soul's long journey through the cycles of life, death, and rebirth. The Akashic Records can teach you a lot about yourself, and can help you to grow. The final chapters of this book will touch on these practices and offer some suggestions for further reading to assist you in continuing to expand the boundaries of your limitless universe.

Astral Projection for Beginners is intended to help you fly beyond the confines of your physical self, showing you how to control the process by offering sound advice on preparation and safety, and providing step-by-step instructions for six different methods of projecting, one of which should work for you.

All it takes now is your desire and perseverance.

PART ONE

UNDERSTANDING
AND PREPARATION

CHAPTER 1

Preparing Yourself to Astral Project, Part 1: Relaxation and Meditation

Forget most of what you've read in bad horror novels and everything you've seen in the movies. You don't need a dark castle turret shrouded in fog and a pointy wizard's hat decorated with lots of glittery stars to be successful at astral projection. The prerequisites are few:

1. A quiet, safe place.

2. A choice of non-tension creating postures.

3. The ability to alter your consciousness.

Creating the Perfect Environment

Though it may seem obvious, it is often overlooked that your astral projection preparations list should begin with the goal of finding a quiet, private place where you can practice. No one enjoys the sensation of being snapped out of an otherwise peaceful meditative or altered state of consciousness, and some practitioners simply do not want to have their interest in astral projection known to anyone else. In other words, intruders and spectators are not welcome.

Worrying about being intruded upon is not conducive to proper relaxation. Sometimes just knowing that someone else knows exactly what it is you're trying to do behind that closed door is enough to keep you from succeeding. Mental censorship is every bit as potent in the astral world as verbal censorship is in the physical. Whether someone approves of what you're doing or not—even if they don't believe it's possible—they can still create thick mental walls you will have to break through in order to succeed. Having your own mental blocks is enough of a hurdle for most of us to handle without taking on those of anyone else.

With the exception of a single trusted working partner, don't give anyone else a chance to stop you before you get started, no matter how tempting such a confidence might be. Keep your astral projection efforts private and, for now, as much of a secret as possible.

Privacy is hard to come by in many homes, and if one of these is yours, you will have to be extra creative when carving out your working space and practice time. Using your own bed just before rising or just before sleeping—

depending on which end of the sleep cycle finds you most alert—can often work in an otherwise crowded household. If this is impossible, or if you find you don't work well reclining in bed, you might have to juggle your daily schedule so you have some other time alone. Or you could choose to work at the home of a trusted partner who is either assisting you in learning astral projection or who is trying to learn right along with you.

Quiet Please!

It is essential to have quiet when you are a beginner at any practice based on successfully altering the state of your consciousness, which includes astral projection. Those with lots of years of experience in the art have developed the enviable skill of being about to shut out almost any outside sounds at will.

Until you reach at least the intermediate skill levels, there is no way around the fact that noises will distract you and keep you rooted in the physical. You may think you live in a quiet neighborhood, but meditation has a way of opening your ears to a new reality. Once you lie down to meditate, you're going to discover just how much that dog in the next yard likes to bark, or how clearly you can hear the basketball being bounced in the neighbor's driveway, and you'll be surprised how many noisy cars constantly race up and down your street.

If you're sound sensitive and find even minor noises distracting, you can ease some of your frustrations by reminding yourself that as you get better at altering your consciousness you will also become better at shutting out the evidence of the physical world. Years before I first began to seriously practice astral projection I knew a *curandera* who could astral project at will no matter how much activity was going on around her.

Curanderas are part of a Mexican-American tradition of gifted healers and seers. The one I knew best would appear to mentally fade out in the middle of a consultation and then, just when everyone was convinced she was paying no attention, she would be clear-eyed again and telling her client about the root of the problem, which she had gleaned astrally from distant times and places.

I used to envy her talent and would despair over my slow progress as every little noise seemed to pull me further from my goal. That was when I learned a valuable lesson about comparing my skills and progress with others. It's never a good idea to try to compete with anyone. Working diligently at your own pace is always the best way to succeed.

To help overcome sound distractions, you can try using the commercial ear plugs easily found at any drug store, or you can play some non-vocal music softly in the background to help block out these sounds. If you want to work with music, be sure to choose instrumental pieces that are flowing and soft. Avoid strong rhythms and all music with lyrics. Strong rhythms and words give your conscious mind something other than the task at hand to latch onto and this can impede your progress. The appendix in the back of this book offers some mail order catalogs that sell music specifically for meditation, if you are interested in trying these.

If you have a room in your home's interior in which to practice away from doors and windows, this will help drown out outside noises but not the internal clunks and clanks. The variety of noises your home or apartment building makes while going about its daily business is a revelation to most beginners at meditation. Your air conditioner, heater, refrigerator, water pumps, etc., all shut off and on at intervals all day and all night. For a novice meditator it can be maddening. At my house, I have a very noisy well pump in the crawl space under the master bedroom that raises my annoyance factor at times. The only thing you can do in this case is to move from room to room, experimenting with each to find the quietest spot.

Keeping the Body Warm

You will need to keep warm while trying to astral project. If you allow your body to get too cold it will be harder to maintain your meditative state. Your fully relaxed and inert body will quickly grow cool, so you might want to cover yourself with an afghan or other lightweight blanket before beginning. On the other hand, you have to be comfortable, so wearing very loose clothing or nothing at all under the covering is advised.

It is speculated that in the distant past people kept warm as they practiced astral projection by stretching out near their fireplaces. In fact, many believe this to be the origin of the Halloween legends of witches "flying" on broomsticks up through the chimney, into the night sky.

Finding the Right Body Posture

Select a physical posture for meditation that you can remain comfortable in for thirty to sixty minutes. This usually means no crossing of the arms or legs unless you generally practice in the Eastern Asian meditative traditions and are accustomed to these types of positions. Crossed arms and legs become uncomfortable for most of us after a short while and this physical discomfort will distract from the focus you will be trying to maintain. Many occultists in the western schools (i.e., European-based) feel that crossed arms and legs impedes the flow of personal energy that you need to be successful.

No matter what you may have been told, no single body position is inherently right or wrong, nor will it affect the overall astral experience you will have. Many people have strong opinions on which body posture is best, based on what has worked best for them. My advice to you is to listen to the pros and cons of all of them, then experiment and draw your own conclusions.

You may choose to lie down or sit up, whichever you prefer. I happen to prefer lying down, but one of my best friends can't project unless she is sitting up in her recliner with her head lolling forward. There is no way I could astral project the way she does, nor could she successfully work my way.

If you choose to sit, it is usually recommended by the advanced practitioners that you attempt to keep your spine as straight as possible to keep the energy flowing through you and to prevent stress-point fatigue from causing discomfort, which can distract you (though this is obviously not a problem for my head-lolling friend).

If you choose to lie down, make sure you are practicing at a time when you are not going to inadvertently fall asleep. Falling asleep while trying to astral project will not harm you, but you will not be successful at consciously projecting if you do. Maintaining an awareness of where your astral consciousness is and controlling its actions is what separates astral projection from dreams and other uncontrolled psychic experiences.

The Eastern mystic schools (East Asian and Indian, for example) have a whole catalog of interesting meditative postures, most of which westerners find hard to either achieve or maintain. These often involve contorting the arms and legs into positions that people conditioned to sitting in hard-backed chairs or plush sofas are not accustomed.

These Eastern occult schools also teach that various positions are best for different types of meditation. If you are already using one or more of these, feel free to select the one you think will work best for your astral projection experiments. If you're not using one of these already, now is not the time to begin. Choosing a posture that is familiar and comfortable is best when beginning to learn astral projection.

Altered States of Consciousness

Successful astral projection does not require a deep meditative state, or what is sometimes called an *altered state of consciousness*, but it does require that you know how to enter and exit one with reasonable ease.

In spite of what Hollywood has tried to impress upon us for dramatic effect, there is no great mystery to this process. It neither contains any inherent danger nor is it something that only the blessed or talented can achieve. The word *altered* merely means "changed"; an altered state of consciousness refers only to a variation or change in the number of brain wave cycles you produce per second. This isn't New Age psycho-babble, but an actual physiological change that is measurable by a medical machine known as an *electroencephalograph*, or EEG. These changes in brain activity levels (BALs) are divided into four broad categories: beta, alpha, theta, and delta.

Brain Activity Level Chart

State	CPS[1]	Definition
beta	15-18	normal waking consciousness used while actively thinking, studying, reasoning, and conversing
alpha	8-12	light to medium altered state used for light to mid-level meditation; also the minimal state needed to succeed at most occult endeavors, including astral projection; includes states of daydreaming, focused non-analytical thought, watching television, light reading, and the sleep level associated with REM, or dream, sleep; waking from this level is not difficult
theta	4-6	deep altered state associated with Zen, other complex occult practices, and mid-level to deep sleep; waking from this level can be moderately difficult or unpleasant

1. Cycles per second.

delta	O.5-2.5	this level characterizes the very deepest levels of sleep and is present when we are in a coma; at this level, there is no awareness of the physical body or its needs, though some people are able to recall details about events and conversations that have take place in the room around them; waking from this state ranges from very difficult to almost impossible

The mid-regions of the alpha level are all that are required to achieve astral projection, though the deeper you can take yourself and the longer you can keep yourself there, the better.

Changes in consciousness, or BALs, happen naturally many times throughout every day of our lives. For example, during a normal night's sleep of eight hours' duration, the human brain will move from alpha to delta and back again approximately five times, with the delta levels becoming shorter each time and the alpha longer.

The simple acts of daydreaming, reading, or watching television will also lower your cycles per second output into the light alpha levels. These are all altered states of consciousness. The only difference between these naturally occurring altered states and deliberate meditation is the fact that you are attempting to control your brain activity rather than allowing it to happen randomly. This is no more dangerous than was your potty training. In both cases, you simply sought to control aspects of your body's functioning.

Learning the Art of Meditation

Aside from being a springboard into a variety of occult practices, including astral projection, people who meditate on a regular basis acquire a host of other benefits. Studies have shown that meditators have lower blood pressure, stronger immune systems, and fewer stress-related illnesses. They tend to sleep better, think quicker, and have higher energy levels than non-meditators. Even if you someday decide you don't want to pursue astral projection any further, learning the art of meditation will forever enhance all these other areas of your life.

There are numerous books, audio tapes, and videos on the market that teach all the nit-picky details of meditation or that focus on a particular method within a specific occult school of thought. These are great to use if meditation alone is your end goal. Presumably you want to learn to astral project, and this requires only an intermediate skill level that, while it still requires practice, does not require a special library from which to learn. Almost anyone can have some success meditating simply by fully relaxing the body and taking control of all conscious thoughts.

Progressive Relaxation

To begin your meditation practice, go to that warm, quiet, private place we already talked about, and then get into a body posture in which you can relax and remain comfortable for at least thirty minutes. Close your eyes and take a few deep, slow breaths. As you exhale, visualize all the tension draining from your body. There will undoubtedly still be some tense spots after you do this, and we will come back and slay these dragons, but for now just relax as much as possible and continue.

Next, you want to do what has been called *progressive relaxation.* This is a meditative trick that allows you to relax your entire body by focusing on its individual points, relaxing each of them thoroughly before continuing on up the body.

When each individual point is mentally isolated like this, its condition becomes clearer and so it becomes easier to relax it than to relax your entire body at once. It's a time-consuming process, but as you do this you will become aware of just how many small pockets of tension you carry around with you on a regular basis.

When I first tried progressive relaxation, I was surprised at the places where clinched muscles were always present, and now, many years later, I still find that if I'm in pain or emotionally upset, these are the areas where I collect tension and where it is hardest to relax. This type of relaxation is also a great technique for helping you fall asleep if you're having trouble drifting off due to a stress-filled day, so it has benefits beyond simple meditation.

Start your progressive relaxation by focusing on your toes. Try to allow no other thoughts to come into your mind other than those surrounding your toes. Mentally will each of them to be totally relaxed. Do this individually, toe by toe, if you must. Focus all of your attention and you will soon notice where the tight areas are— where you have cramped muscles and where you are having trouble letting go and relaxing completely. Some people like to accompany this process with mental visualizations where they can "see" the tension draining away from the part of the body being relaxed. You might want to see the tension dissolve away like sugar in water, or watch it break up and fade away into the ground beneath you, or see a wave of warm, relaxing water wash over it. Choose whatever imagery most strongly represents relaxation to you—this is what will best assist your efforts.

When you have fully relaxed your toes, move your awareness on up to your feet and go through the same process. You don't need to spend more than thirty or forty-five seconds on each body part unless you sense an extraordinary amount of tension hovering there.

After the toes and feet, move your awareness on up to your ankles, the shins, the knees, etc., until you have worked up to the top of your head. Pay extra attention to areas of the body in which we all tend to collect tension, such as the shoulders, back of the neck, jaw, and forehead. Also pay attention to any areas in which you often experience pain. These are areas where the muscles are likely to be tighter. For example, if you are an athlete and often have sore joints, or if you suffer from carpal tunnel syndrome due to working with repetitive motions, the muscles corresponding to those areas are likely to be extra tense.

Focusing Your Will

Once you feel fully relaxed, take another deep breath and begin to focus your thoughts on one thing only. If you tend to be a visually-oriented person who "sees" your ideas, then you might want to pick an image or symbol to hold in your mind. Keep the shape, color, and texture very simple for now.

If, on the other hand, you are someone aurally-oriented, who "hears" ideas rather than sees them, you might want to pick a phrase (often called a mantra when you are meditating) to repeat over and over to yourself. Keep the phrase short, generic, and related to your ultimate goal—your reason for wanting to alter your consciousness in the first place. In this instance, you might want to repeat, "I astral project, I astral project," over and over to yourself.

Be sure to keep your affirmation positive and in the present tense. In these lower altered states the mind becomes very receptive, which is one reason why the idea of sleep learning has gone through periods of popularity, and if you make your statement in the future tense you may end up keeping your goal in the future as well.

Make sure you state your phrase as if it is already a fact in your life. Again, keep it positive—don't focus on the negatives, like "I will stop thinking I can't astral project," or "I will not be afraid of astral projection." See how these statements focus on negative aspects of your goal rather than on positive ones? To dwell on them only feeds your self-doubt by tossing negative energy into your practice. If you really want to overcome those things that stand in your way (and we all have or have had some of these at some point), then simply make an affirmation that already sees your success as part of your current reality.

Another purpose of this affirmation is to convince all levels of your mind of their truth. We've all read enough studies on the brain-mind-body connection to have some understanding of the ways in which we help shape our own reality. Once the mind is convinced of something there is little that can stop the rest of your being from following through.

Holding onto one single thought is not as easy as it sounds, and in the beginning your mind will want to wander off and seek out something more entertaining to do. This is the point where many people give up in frustration. Resist the urge to quit, or even to stop and tell yourself you'll start again tomorrow. This only lets that resistant part of your mind win the battle and, like a spoiled child, it will only cry all the louder next time you do what it doesn't like until you give into it again. This starts you on a downward spiral of failure that can be hard to overcome later on when you finally figure out where you first went wrong.

Whenever your mind wanders away from your goal, just firmly pull it back to the thoughts you want it to have and continue as if nothing happened. Slowly work your way up to where you can hold a single thought for at least ten minutes. Keep in mind that you will be unaware of the passage of time while you're meditating, so remember to look at a clock or watch just before and just after each session to check your progress.

Creating a Dramatic Scenario

Once you have mastered this part of the meditation art, which may take a few weeks or a few months depending on your previous experience and your efforts, the next step is getting into your meditative state and allowing a dramatic scene to form in your mind.

Choose a scenario you find irresistible and let it unfold in front of your inner eyes as if it were being projected onto a 360-degree movie screen.

This is your chance to enter the best kind of virtual reality there is—a chance to live out your greatest desire. There are no limitations. Make yourself the star, writer, and director, and then give yourself an Oscar. The sensation you will experience while doing this in a controlled meditative state is similar to what you will experience while astral projecting, and often the mere practice of seeing yourself in these scenes will actually place you there so you can take off and project anywhere else you want to go (see chapter 8).

I have discovered that people who have always had vivid imaginations and rich fantasy lives do best with astral projection. There is definitely a connection between the two, so start developing your inner world now if you haven't already.

Mental Counting

Mental counting is another popular method for achieving or deepening an altered state of consciousness. This is usually done by counting down numbers to yourself in order to enter into the altered state, and then counting back up again when you're ready to exit. It is lulling to the mind, and is similar to counting sheep to overcome insomnia.

Mental counting helps many people relax and achieve a receptive state of mind. The numbers you choose to begin and end with are up to you, and can be combined with your controlled breathing (see next page) if this helps you focus. You can also repeat a set of numbers over and over again to yourself. For instance, if you are part of an occult tradition that treats seven as a sacred number, as many Christian mystic schools do, or even if it is just your personal lucky number based on experience or numerology, then you might want to count down from seven to one over and over to enter your meditation and up from one to seven to exit.

Chanting

Using chanting to assist you is just another way of using a mantra, or a rhythmic affirmation repeated verbally or mentally over and over while the mind focuses on its deeper meaning. Transformational chanting, or chanting used to change one condition into another, is ancient in origin, and it has again become popular among New Agers, modern shamans, Pagans, and in women's spirituality settings. For your purposes at this time it's best to select a short, simple phrase related to your goal, such as "I astral project," or "I fly." As with your previous affirmation, keep it short, positive, and in the present tense.

The Power of Controlled Breathing

One of the most basic of all meditative practices is controlled breathing, a skill elevated to a high spiritual art in the East Asian and Vedic mystic traditions. To mimic this, you will need to allow the natural rhythm of your breathing to lull you into a deeper altered state as you meditate.

The world is just now rediscovering the increased mental stimulation and other health benefits brought about by proper breathing, probably because a few savvy folks have found ways to make it profitable. In

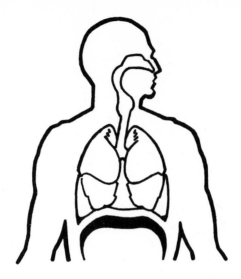

Figure 1. Diaphragm When Inhaling

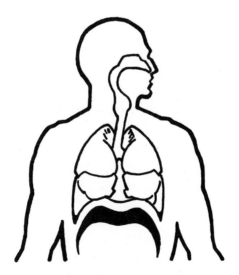

Figure 2. Diaphragm When Exhaling

trendy Los Angeles you can now go to oxygen bars to drink in clean air as you discuss your latest corporate raid. Professional athletes are rushing to hire breathing coaches who they feel will show them the secrets of getting the best performances from their bodies by altering the way they breathe, and a book by holistic fitness guru Pam Grout, *Jump Start Your Metabolism with the Power of Breath* (SkillPath, 1997), promises dramatic weight loss merely by learning proper deep breathing techniques.

Profitable or not, breathing correctly is important to your goal of astral projection. One of the ways newcomers to altered state work impede their own progress is by improper breathing. This concept sounds silly to many people who think breathing is so natural that no one should have to be taught, but that's not so. Healthy breathing is natural, deep breathing that comes from the diaphragm and not the chest. The diaphragm is an elongated muscle below the lungs that is responsible for expanding and contracting them. When you take a deep breath it is the diaphragm muscle you are moving, not the lungs themselves.

Take a moment now to take note of the way you breathe. Does your diaphragm area move or is your breathing shallow and centered in the upper chest? Now take a few slow, deep breaths. Is your mid-section near your diaphragm doing most of the expanding and contracting, or are you forcing this task in your chest? How about the position of your shoulders? When you are standing or sitting and your shoulders rise and fall with each breath you take, you are doing something wrong. The shoulders should remain perfectly still when you breathe.

This huffing and puffing and calling it deep breathing is a common mistake we all learned in kindergarten. Observe children being asked to take a deep breath and watch how they make a big show of it by swelling up their chests and puffing out their cheeks. None of their effort is centered where it needs to be. As adults we fall back on these bad breathing habits to enhance our vanity. Both men and women tend to want to keep the stomach area flat and understated while accenting the chest. In truth, a strong diaphragm will help pull in the stomach muscles, not accentuate them.

Most people are forced to breathe correctly if they are lying down flat on their backs. If you are unsure of whether you're breathing from your diaphragm or not, try lying down on a hard surface and notice how your upper stomach area, and not your chest, tends to rise and fall the most.

The other time that people breathe right is while sleeping. Everyone breathes correctly during sleep unless an illness or other physical problem causes interference. Take some time to watch a sleeper breathe. Notice the slow, deep intake of air from the solar plexus area, not from the chest. Professional singers also know how to breathe correctly since diaphragm breathing is essential to controlling the phrasing of songs and producing powerful voices.

If you are trying to alter your consciousness through basic meditation and find that your mind still tends to wander, you may want to try counting each breath as it comes to you. Try this on both the exhale and then on the inhale to see if it makes a difference in the way you feel.

It is standard occult practice to inhale through your nose and exhale through your mouth when doing deliberate deep breathing exercises. This is a common practice in occult schools of India and Eastern Asia, where this is believed to set up an unimpeded flow of energy through the body that is easily drawn from for practices like astral projection. There are also health benefits to this type of breathing. The follicles and membranes in your nose help filter out impurities and warm the air before it enters your lungs.

You can also try altering your breathing patterns to see what affect they have on your consciousness. By patterns, I mean the "beats" or counts taken for inhaling, pausing, exhaling, and pausing again. When awake and relaxed, most of us inhale for two beats, pause for a half beat, then exhale for two beats and pause for another half beat before inhaling again.

A beat is not a fixed amount of time, though most people have a sense of what it means. Sometimes stage and television scripts will use the term *beat* in their stage direction to the actors to denote a small gap of time between lines or actions. This is especially true in comedies, where timing is essential to having a line come across as funny or causing it to fall with a slam. My own idea of a beat is something just a fraction less than a single second, but if your idea of a beat runs for a second and a half you're still in the right area.

One popular meditation breathing pattern is inhaling for five beats, holding the breath for three beats, exhaling for five beats, then holding that for three beats, and so forth. I've also tried using a four/one/four/one pattern and found that it is a good one to use with astral projections whose goal is to explore spirit worlds. A three/one/three/one or a two/two/two/two also have images they set up in my mind that seems to set expectations for astral exploration. The first tends to be one that lets me explore elemental kingdoms where faery beings and the basic building blocks of existence dwell, and the latter usually puts me in a frame of mind to meet with old astral friends.

As you fall more deeply into your astral projection you will start to lose track of your breathing pattern and it will find its own balance based on what you're doing in the astral world. Don't expect to have to worry about your breathing for the entire experiment.

I once read a book on meditation that advised against experimenting with breathing patterns because they were actually a psychic code that could possibly attract something undesirable your way. That sort of alarmist thinking has no place in positive occultism. Most ancient cultures taught that the breath was sacred, a means by which life was sustained and through which life was preserved, if the breath was captured by a tribal shaman. If there is any code at work, it is simply that of your own inner being and finding what pattern resonates best with your intention to learn astral projection. Don't be afraid to experiment. If you do happen to find a breathing pattern that makes you feel uncomfortable in any way, simply change it to one you like better.

Also, keep in mind the distinction between proper deep breathing and using breathing patterns. They are two different concepts. Proper deep breathing—breathing deeply from the diaphragm—is essential to good altered state work. Using specific breathing patterns is very helpful to many practitioners, but it is not absolutely essential. A few people, especially westerners, may find using patterned breathing more distracting than helpful, and those with asthma or other respiratory problems might find them difficult.

Leaving the Meditative State

When you are ready to stop meditating, simply begin to get a sense of your physical body once more. Do this by taking the focus off your meditation and turning it onto your physical body. Begin to think about your head, your face, your neck, etc., and remember what it is to be a corporeal being again.

It is also recommended that you try, whenever possible, to come out of the meditative state using the same process by which you entered. This keeps your analytical mind—which always craves order and logic—happy so that it can keep in sync with your creative mind, and allows for a smooth transition of thought and mental images. When you feel solidly back in the physical, you may open your eyes and begin to move your body.

At this point many people like to do something very physical to make clearer the separation between the meditative world and the physical one. It need not be an elaborate gesture. You can just stomp your feet, shout, or eat. Or you can have safe sex, run a few miles, enjoy an aerobic workout, or do anything else that a living, corporeal being can do. Get your blood moving and your heart pounding. This is the time to revel in the fact that you're alive and fully a part of the physical world.

CHAPTER 2

Preparing Yourself to Astral Project, Part 2: The Chakras and Other "Secrets"

Aside from the obvious prerequisites, such as being relaxed and having the ability to alter your level of consciousness at will, there are a host of other ways to increase your chances of successful astral projection, or to enhance the astral experiences you may already be having. These bolstering forces include astral journaling, chakra work, drawing on other energies for assistance, and using weather conditions or astrological phenomena for enhancement. I'll address each in this chapter.

Keeping Your Astral Journal

At this point in your study of astral projection it's time to get serious about keeping records of your experiences and progress. The importance of journaling occult experiences, especially in the beginning stages, is often not apparent until it's too late to go back and recreate all the notes that should have been made.

Your astral journal does not need to be fancy, though some people like to make or purchase elegantly bound books with blank pages. A spiral-bound or loose-leaf notebook works perfectly. I prefer the loose-leaf so I can organize material in the way that I like to study it. Instead of having everything in chronological order, I organize by failures and successes, then have my successes ordered by the type of astral projection that was experienced: spirit contact, knowledge quest, karmic questions, etc. You might also want to arrange your pages based on astrological events, weather conditions, noise levels, or anything else that might affect your overall experience. If you do start out with a spiral-bound notebook I recommend that it be one that has perforated pages and a three-hole punch so that it can be disassembled and transferred into a loose-leaf journal if you decide this is what you want later on.

The purpose of having a journal of some kind to record your astral projection progress is threefold. First of all, it helps you to identify the conditions that are most conducive to your personal success. For example, you may find you are best able to astral project when the moon is in the sign of Pisces or when there is a pouring rain. You might also find you are at your worst while burning jasmine incense or when there is an electrical storm approaching. Pick one day each month to look back over your journal and take note of all the different entries with an objective eye. Over time you will see the pattern of your own affinities emerging and will know which ones to take advantage of when they present themselves.

Secondly, your astral journal gives you an accurate representation of your ratio of success to failure, so you can more accurately chart your progress. Lastly, it helps you put all of your astral experiences in perspective. In your journal, you can make notes of knowledge gained or beings met while on your astral journeys so you can better get an idea of where you are growing spiritually, which should be the main focus of the majority of your astral projections.

You should also note in your journal any fluctuations in your emotional state or general health. Even the slightest change in either area could make a big difference in your ability to project or in the quality of that projection. It should go without saying that you should not attempt to astral project if you are sick, angry, or upset. The latter two are negative emotions that will only be compounded in a realm where thought is made manifest at the speed of light. Astral projection takes a tremendous reserve of personal energy for beginners. Under normal conditions you are unlikely to ever feel truly depleted after a projection, but if your body's energy reserves are engaged in fighting an illness, you will only make yourself sicker if you try projecting at this time. I learned this lesson the hard way and turned a few sniffles into one of the most miserable colds I ever had to endure, complete with a three-day bout of laryngitis.

Below is a sample entry form for you to copy and modify for use in your own astral journal. Please note that the final entry is to be used for making notes at some future date when you've had time to mull over the astral experience and put it into perspective with regard to your overall spiritual goals.

Sample Astral Journal Entry

DATE:

START TIME: STOP TIME:

PHYSICAL LOCATION:

PERSONAL HEALTH NOTES:

PURPOSE OF THIS PROJECTION:

WEATHER NOTES:

ASTROLOGICAL DATA:

ASSISTANCE USED (IF ANY):

   MUSIC: PRAYERS:

   SCENT: CANDLES:

   COLORS: OINTMENTS:

   OTHER:

METHOD OF ALTERED STATE INDUCTION:

DESCRIPTION OF PROJECTION EXPERIENCE:

ANY BEINGS MET:

APPARENT ROLE OF THOSE BEINGS:

NATURE OF INTERACTION WITH OTHERS ON THE ASTRAL PLANE:

WHAT I LEARNED FROM THIS PROJECTION:

LATER INSIGHTS　　　　　DATE NOTES MADE:

TRUE PURPOSE:

WHAT WAS LEARNED:

WHAT WORKED AND WHAT DIDN'T:

THE TRUE ROLE OF BEINGS ENCOUNTERED:

OTHER NOTES:

The Role of Chakras in Astral Projection

Another meditation practice that not only aids astral projection but enhances other occult endeavors and psychic abilities is one where the chakras, or energy centers, of the body are stimulated and opened.

There are seven major chakra centers along the body, which correspond to different mental, emotional, and physical functions of the body. See Figure 3 on the facing page for the positioning of the chakras. Most people are unaware that psychic messages and energy pass in and out of these energy centers every day. We can catch hints of this awareness in our metaphoric language when we talk about something feeling like a punch in the stomach, or making the heart ache, or causing the throat to tighten, or having a gut feeling. These areas of the body correspond to chakra centers.

The chakras also function as portals between our physical selves and the astral world. Whenever one or more of the chakras is not functioning properly, or whenever it's fully closed or fully opened at the wrong time, a slowing of spiritual progress or physical illness can be the result.

Balancing and Cleansing the Chakras

Doing a chakra cleansing exercise prior to projecting is especially useful if you plan to use one of these centers as an exit point for astral projecting (see chapter 6). Cleansing will make it easier to draw in the energy you need to help you be successful. If you are interested in learning the art of remote healing (see chapter 12), or the practice of healing someone else while in a projected state, learn to do this chakra cleansing well, for it will form the basis for your future healing efforts. Balancing and cleansing

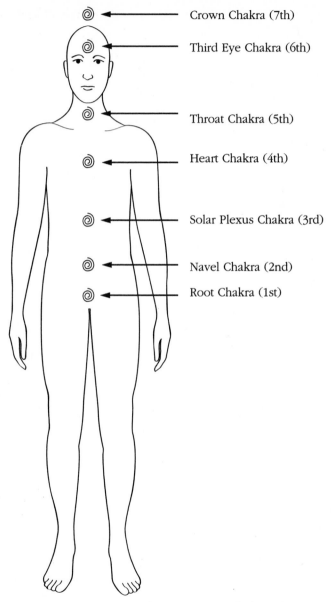

Crown Chakra (7th)

Third Eye Chakra (6th)

Throat Chakra (5th)

Heart Chakra (4th)

Solar Plexus Chakra (3rd)

Navel Chakra (2nd)

Root Chakra (1st)

Figure 3. The Seven Major Chakras

the chakra areas is also beneficial for mental and physical health, and for a variety of occult practices.

While in your meditative state, visualize each one of the chakras individually. Start from the root, or base, chakra and work your way up. The root chakra is red in color. Visualize it as a vivid sphere that expands and opens at your will, allowing for the free exchange of beneficial energy. Mentally remove any spots, blotches, or dark patches that seem to indicate blockages or damage to the chakra. Use visualization in any way that helps you to accomplish this. When you are done with the root chakra, move on up the body to the next chakra until all seven are complete. When you are done, each should be seen pure and clear as if they are living beings in and of themselves.

Color Associations for Chakras

Chakra	Color
root	red
navel	orange
solar plexus	yellow
heart center	green
throat	blue
third eye	indigo
crown	violet

Before you end your meditation or astral projection, partially close down each chakra you've opened, starting from the crown and moving to the root. You do not want them fully open and receiving uncontrolled energies throughout the day, but you do not want them completely closed for health reasons.

Using Music as a Chakra Stimulant

If you find you're having trouble opening your chakras, there is a trick that can help you: using music as an inducement or, more specifically, using specific notes of the scale. Each of the twelve tones of the scale contains its own energy pattern that, when it collides with your unique chemical, spiritual, and physical makeup, can affect or influence you toward a certain emotional or mental mindset. In India and east Asia, this art, which is sometimes called by the cumbersome and unsatisfactory term *chromaticology* among western New Agers, has been known for centuries. Chromaticology attempts to catalog and utilize the effects of music on the psyche.

Each tone of the scale is believed to relate to a specific chakra, which will respond by becoming energized, balanced, and open.

Corresponding Musical Notes for Chakras

Chakra	Corresponding Note
root	C
navel	D
solar plexus	E
heart center	F
throat	G
third eye	A
crown	B

The other five tones of the scale, known as the chromatics (C-sharp, E-flat, F-sharp, G-sharp, and B-flat), can be used to open the energy centers of other parts of the body and awaken the astral (emotional), spiritual, or mental bodies. Which ones work best for which area vary depending on the school of thought you study and your personal affinities. If you want to seriously begin working with music as a spiritual tool, I recommend that you record (or have a partner who can play) various sustained tones while you are in deep meditation, allowing you to experiment with what works best for you. Be sure to record your findings, along with any other pertinent information about each specific session, in your astral journal or other record book so you can see your own pattern emerging.

I discovered my own music-chakra pattern early in my occult experiments, probably because I began studying music about the same time I was learning to read, and music has always been a part of both my inner and outer life. I found that the note D induces in me feelings of personal power and triumph, and so this is a note I sound when I become unsure in my astral travels. E and C-sharp open my mind to deeper mysteries and are very good for helping me to understand my Akashic Records (see chapter 11). B-flat tends to make me depressed if I work with it too long and can put me at risk of attracting undesirable lower astral beings (see chapter 3), and G-sharp sends me on inner world nostalgia trips.

When doing your own musical experiments, don't stop at single notes. Feel free to combine them, even the ones that sound less pleasing to your ears. You might be surprised at the effect. You can also try playing with the octave in which each note is sounded. For instance, an F below middle C may influence you differently than the F above high C.

Music is a powerful tool for spiritual development, especially in helping you open to astral projection. Most people are aware of the power that music has to tug at the emotions. How many times have you heard an old song, one you may not have listened to for years, but all of a sudden you find that it bombards you with vivid memories? This is because it acts directly on the emotional center of your brain and, through the brain, can stimulate your astral body—which is, after all, also known as your *emotional* body.

You may need to experiment with a variety of sounds, textures, and sensations to find out what stimulates your own chakras.

Drawing on Other Energies for Assistance

Aside from the preparations already discussed, there are dozens of other things you can do for yourself that may or may not help you to be successful. None of these are absolutely necessary, and you may find you do very well projecting without them. Others find they enjoy the props both to draw on their inherent energies and for their aesthetic qualities. These include the use of incenses, ointments, or oils, which have long been known in occult circles to help the consciousness to escape from the confines of the body.

Other types of assistance can be described more as personal quirks than ancient secrets. Almost all successful astral projectors have a few of these, and they work time and time again for those who swear by them. For example, some people say they can successfully project only when their head is in the north; when they have their hands placed right over left; when they are wearing a spiritual or religious symbol with lots of personal meaning; when they have jasmine oil on their foreheads; when they are lying on a special pillow; when they wear their favorite clothes; when they do ten sit-ups first; when they take a bath with peach petals; etc. This list is only the tip of the proverbial iceberg of quirks I've heard people confess to having. Most of these things work very well for the people who use them because they believe they work, and belief is the key to succeeding at any occult endeavor.

Natural Magic

Other practices have their roots in the ancient art of *natural magic*. Natural magic asserts that all things in nature have energy patterns that can be drawn on to assist us in attaining specific goals and needs. These techniques are not just for the neo-Pagans and New Agers, but are based on the folk practices and beliefs of the common people of all cultures and religions. The energy patterns in nature and in the color spectrum are there to help us, if we will let them.

Candles. You might want to burn a blue candle while you try to project to take advantage of both the energy of fire and of the peaceful, dream-inducing energies of the color blue. Violet candles also work in this same way, and many astral projectors swear by them.

Candles provide us with a pleasant medieval occult atmosphere and can enhance the psychic environment when we try to astral project. If you choose to use candles as an aid, please be aware of the dangers of having an open, unattended fire burning in your house. Make sure your working partner is aware of them or, if you have no partner, see that they are sitting somewhere where they cannot possibly cause damage if they are knocked over. I often set mine in the stainless steel kitchen sink or on the floor of the ceramic tiled shower stall for this reason.

Incense. Incense contained in a special burner is less of a danger than an open candle flame. Their scents can not only help provide energy on which you can draw, but the smell can help reduce outside smells that might distract you from your goal. Jasmine or sandalwood are good choices for astral projection incense. They possess the right energies you need to draw from and they are easy to find.

If you don't think smells can distract just as much as noise, try experimenting with scents to see just how easily they evoke memories or feelings. For example, strong cooking odors coming from your neighbor's apartment will not help you relax and focus, but will only keep your mind on the physical—either on your upcoming meal or on that wonderful pecan pie your grandmother used to make.

Essential Oils. Essential oils are volatile oils that are extracted from herbs and plants. When placed on the chakras, they can be used to stimulate and open them so the chakras can be used as portals to the astral world. Some caution must be used with these oils, since many of them can cause skin irritation. Lilac oil is often used if the purpose of the projection is the viewing of past lives, and sage helps to evoke scenes of future events. For general astral projection try experimenting with jasmine, gardenia, rose or bay oil.

Herbs. Small pillows stuffed with herbs whose scents and energies can be drawn on to assist projection have also been employed. Any small pouch of simple cotton cloth can be used for this. It need not be fancy, or even be sewn together, as long as it can be wrapped up to hold the herbs in a way that is similar to how most people tie a garbage bag.

Some people place this pouch under their bed pillow before projection attempts. Others hold it in their lap or place it over or near a specific chakra. Experiment to find what works best for you. The best herb to use for stuffing this pillow is mugwort, an ingredient often seen in "flying ointments" or formulas, which will be discussed later. Others that work well are bay, honeysuckle, wormwood, eyebright, valerian, and lemongrass. Refer to the appendix for suppliers who sell the herbs, oils, and incenses mentioned in this chapter.

Keep in mind as you work through this chapter that everyone's psyche is a little bit different. It pays to spend the time finding out what works best for you, not just for overall assistance in astral projection, but for each particular method of astral projection. It's possible that the herbal scent that best helps you project using the guided meditation method may not be the best for using the symbolic gateway method.

The Influence of Weather and Astrology

Many occult writings, both contemporary and ancient, allude to the importance of weather or to the use of astrological phenomena for success in astral projection. As with many other aspects of this art, these "sure things" are usually in conflict with one another, though many practitioners today swear by one or another.

I have known people who believe that starting to learn astral projection on the full moon is best, while others say the dark aspects of the new moon are better. Some like to draw energy from the highly charged atmosphere of an electrical storm, and others say only calm, clear weather works for them.

The point is that we all have different affinities and idiosyncrasies, and no doubt all of these events work best for someone. Whether that someone is you is something that only you can decide. These discrepancies are another of the reasons why teachers of the occult strongly recommend that new students keep a journal of their practices, including notations on the moon's phase and astrological sign, air temperature, weather conditions, and any other pertinent information that affects either the psychic or physical atmosphere.

Astral Controversies

You may have noticed that all the types of astral projection assistance mentioned so far involve things that remain external in relation to the body. When we start talking about things that can be taken internally we find ourselves in the middle of an age-old occult debate. When we take drugs whose purpose is to alter our consciousness for us we rob ourselves of the learning process. There is no skill needed to take a pill as a shortcut into an altered state.

Some argue that they use only herbs for this purpose, not real drugs, but we are still dealing with a chemical change in the body that comes as the result of some-thing we take rather than something we do because we are skilled. When you can cause that same chemical change by willing it, you are in control of your entire being and capable of doing almost anything you want inside or outside.

I recommend that you learn to project without the assistance of ingested drugs or herbs, and then if you ever need help relaxing, take only the mildest relaxing herbal formula you can to help you get into the right frame of mind and to open the psychic centers. Other-wise these "aids" will quickly become a crutch you can-not move without.

Many newcomers to altered state work are surprised to learn that they can inadvertently create crutches they later have trouble discarding. Anything you become dependent on to lull you into an altered state can become addictive and, therefore, destructive in terms of your building the occult skills you want to be able to call on at will.

On one hand you want your pre-altered state rituals to have enough uniformity to trigger your mind to become aware that a change will be taking place. In metaphysi-cal terms, this is the very nature of ritual: to use symbol-ism in such a way that it evokes a response from your psyche, sending it in your desired direction.

But, on the other hand, you want to make sure you remain in control of the ritual, and not the other way around. I know a man who used the same piece of New Age music every time he attempted to meditate, no mat-ter what the goal of the meditation. Only a year later he confessed to me that he found himself unable to achieve an altered state of consciousness without that specific piece of music.

I nearly did myself the same disservice by overusing sandalwood incense. I love the scent of true sandalwood so much that it was the only one I would select for my early efforts. Fortunately, I realized the damage I was doing when I went to a group astral projection experiment at the home of a friend who was using frankincense incense. I immediately began to alternate the things I used at home. To this day the scent of sandalwood invokes an almost instant alpha state in me, so I use it sparingly. But it's nice to know that I can count on its help if all other efforts fail.

In Part 2 of this book, I offer suggestions for incense, teas, oils, and other substances that I feel may help you to learn certain astral projection techniques or help open you to specific regions of the astral plane. These suggestions are based on the known occult properties of the substances as well as on my own personal experiences. You should feel free to experiment with other substances as your skills develop. Vary them to find combinations that you can rely on and that help you avoid the dependency trap.

The point of this digression is not to tell you to avoid those things that can help you learn occult arts like astral projection, or to exclude those that can help you achieve your goals on the occasional times when the effort seems more difficult. The point is simply to show you how to exercise caution and common sense so that you can achieve all that you wish to achieve. True power comes from within. Don't give it away by becoming dependent on anything outside of yourself.

Confusing Concepts

Although we do know that power comes from within, there is nothing wrong with allowing external circumstances to trigger your mind to recognize that a change is about to take place—or even to help send it on its way, as long as you are controlling the process. This is what any good pre-astral projection ritual should do. The moment you begin preparing your work area in your usual way, or assume a familiar posture, you should feel yourself automatically begin to slip into an altered state of consciousness. This is part of what you're striving toward and you don't want to ruin it by panicking that you have started an addiction.

As long as the "addiction" is coming from you—things you do, ways you move or sit, etc.—you are developing what occultists call a *ritual consciousness*, and it only proves that you're growing in your skill level.

What you *don't* want is to be dependent on a specific scent or sound that is completely out of your control. A good test is to ask yourself, "If I were alone on a desert island, would I have everything with me that I need in order to feel that I could successfully astral project?" If the answer is no, it's time to reevaluate your system.

Those Mysterious Flying Ointments

Many books on astral projection and practical occultism discuss the making and using of flying ointments, greasy formulas reputed to be ancient in origin, which have the reputation for assisting the astral body to separate from the physical. The ointment is applied liberally to the entire body prior to attempting astral projection.

to have energies helpful to astral projection. Research your ingredients thoroughly to make sure that the substance is not irritating, poisonous, or one that causes an allergic reaction; you just may find something that works very well for you, even though others would find it useless.

Whatever quirks you develop for your own astral projecting sessions, or whichever aids you use to try to assist you, remember that *you* are the source of the power, not the props you use. Living a healthy lifestyle, being in a positive frame of mind, and your honest efforts are what count the most. These are what will ultimately allow you to succeed.

Astral Projection Preparation in Summary

These opening chapters may have been confusing for those of you who are still new to altered state of consciousness work. What it all really means when applied to astral projection is that only two things are absolutely required of you: 1) the ability to slow the cycles per second of your brain waves—what we call meditating—and 2) that you have a quiet, comfortable place that is private, and where you feel safe.

Ultimately, what you want to do is to be able to condition your mind to allow you to project at will. The less outside assistance you have to use, the greater your skill level. Many people who project successfully need no more than a quiet place, but many others need some extra help, which is where all the herbs, oils, and other accoutrements come in handy. Try projecting first without them. Give it a fair chance. Practice daily for at least a month, then, if you feel you need assistance, add just one other element. For instance, try adding some soft music to drown out outside noises and help slow your mind. Give it another month and, if you still need help, try adding just one other element, like incense. Once you gain some mastery of the art, try taking away one element at a time in the opposite order in which you added them. With practice, you will be able to discipline your mind to project virtually any time or place that you will it to do so.

CHAPTER 3

Travel Safety and Conquering Fear

Astral projection is not appreciably riskier than simply having a dream, and is considerably safer than stepping out of your own front door—yet most beginners are preconditioned to feel fear at the prospect of projecting. These feelings are likely a product of horror films depicting dramatized events that have little or no connection to actual occult practices.

Common sense and lack of fear are the keys to safe travel. One of the laws governing the astral world is that like energies attract like energies. Fear will only attract fearful experiences, so it needs to be dealt with before you begin your astral sojourns.

The first thing to remember is that you are always in control of the astral projection event, at least if you are not under the influence of strong drugs or herbal mixtures. Where you go, whom you interact with, and when and how you return to normal consciousness are all always at your discretion.

Even with that in mind, many people who say they desperately want to learn to astral project will hold back and block their own progress due to a host of fears they've latched onto concerning being in the projected state. These usually fall into one of three categories, each of which we will address in this chapter:

1. Fear of encountering harmful spirits.

2. Fear that the physical body could be harmed while the astral body is elsewhere.

3. Fear of becoming lost on the astral plane or somehow being unable to return to the physical body.

Fear of Encountering Harmful Beings

The beings you might encounter on the astral plane are generally: 1) those native to the higher astral realm, or 2) those native to the lower astral realm. It's important to remember that the designations "lower" and "higher" have nothing to do with actual placement in time or space, but with *vibration* levels.

The concept of spiritual vibration is hard to describe in physical terms. It refers to a frequency inherent in each astral being (including ourselves when we are in the astral world) that determines its spiritual level. Higher frequencies vibrate at a faster rate than lower (slower) frequencies, and are associated with more advanced beings. On the astral plane, like attracts like; beings with higher frequencies attract other high frequency beings while creating an atmosphere hostile to lower frequency beings.

This concept is probably best understood when compared to radio waves. An individual radio frequency can only be "picked up" by someone tuned into that frequency, such as when you tune into a specific radio station. You will never pick up a station broadcasting on a lower frequency if you are spending your time at the other end of the dial tuning into higher frequencies. The same is true of spiritual frequencies. Higher vibrations belong to the more highly evolved or more spiritual beings, and lower frequencies to the less evolved or lower astral beings.

Because the higher frequencies vibrate at a faster rate, the higher vibrating beings are able to enter astral space which is less dense than the areas that can only be reached by beings vibrating at a lower frequency. Though the differences between the higher and lower astral worlds are not really spatial in their differentiation, it is true that the lower astral levels have a feeling of denseness not found in the higher regions. When something vibrates quickly it is able to move through more atmospheres, similar to the way an electric saw moving very fast (higher vibration) can cut through things that a slower (lower vibration) saw cannot.

This is why it's so important to go into the astral world without carrying negative baggage or emotional turmoil.

In a place where thought is action, and where your own vibration rate determines where you can go and whom you meet, it makes sense to carry into the experience only the most positive thoughts and intentions.

This does not mean that you must adhere to some arbitrary set of morals created for you by the society in which you live, but rather that you maintain a high standard of personal ethics in which spiritual advancement for yourself, and the harming of no one else in the process, is the creed you live by. Most spiritual systems have some type of law that addresses this, similar to Christianity's Golden Rule or the Harm None Rede of neo-Paganism. When your vibration rate is high, the entities you encounter will likely be high as well.

Negative feelings and energies that weigh down your vibration rate can be largely eliminated before you enter the astral world. In the early stages of your meditation process, before you actually start to astral project, allow your nervous tension, random thoughts, angers, hatred, prejudices, etc., to be what we call "grounded." This means to visualize them flowing from you into the earth. Or you can mentally bury them or box them, or see them breaking up and falling away from you, or whatever other mental imagery it takes to raise your vibration rate and keep those less than positive thoughts from manifesting in this fluid world that you're about to enter.

Keep in mind as you travel that while the astral may ultimately be in the mind, it is still a very real place and the beings who live there are real too. They all have personalities and feelings that can be trampled on if you're not considerate of them. Chances are that you will not be overly troubled by lower astral entities, but any astral being's ire can be aroused if you slam into its home turf as if you just staged a military coup and you are the new dictator.

You'll also find that you'll keep away the lower astral beings and maintain the good will of the higher ones if you have only positive intentions for being there in the first place. Don't go into the astral with the intent of spying on other people's lives, reading their soul records (see chapter 11), or working with negative intent against a real or imagined enemy. Such negative practices will rebound on you quickly in both the astral and physical worlds.

No one has adequately defined just what a lower astral entity really is or where it was created, but most of us who have projected a lot have seen a few. Some call them fallen angels, others say they are no more than the capricious denizens of the astral we know as faeries. Others claim them to be uncontrolled thoughtforms, or human discarnates (ghosts), who cannot yet move on to other incarnations, while still others call them demons. There is no formulaic way to recognize most of them, but anytime you feel uncomfortable in the presence of someone you meet in the astral, or you find a being physically or psychically attacking you, it's time to get away.

To get away, you can just move your astral body away from the being and hope it doesn't follow you. If that doesn't work you can arm yourself (remember, thought is action!) and visualize whatever weapon you feel will fight off the being. Items representing the protective element of fire, such as flaming swords, white hot knives, or religious icons having meaning to you, work very well. You can also will yourself to be immediately somewhere else while still remaining on the astral plane. Usually the lower astral being cannot make the transition from place to place as quickly as you can and will have trouble following. This is especially true if you move into a region where the vibrational rate is higher and therefore incompatible with your attacker. To make this transition to the higher astral, visualize positive spiritual thoughts as you mentally will yourself to these higher regions. Don't give in to your feelings of anger at this point since this is a negative emotion that could keep you in the lower astral world.

In any of these situations it is best not to will yourself immediately back home—to your physical self—in case the being tries to follow you there. If you do come home, either by choice or accident, immediately visualize the portal between the astral world and the physical one slamming shut and visualize whatever guardians you need to feel that the portal is safely guarded from being used again. The next few times you astral project, make sure you use a different gateway (see chapters 5-10) just in case that being is waiting for you at the familiar one.

Another way to help you gauge the intent of any astral being you meet is simply to gaze at it for a few moments with a critical eye. Just as your thoughts and emotions take shape on the astral plane, so do those of other beings. A dark aura, dark tentacles, or negative imagery emanating from any being is a danger sign. A friend of mine who was dealing with an alcoholic husband saw this clearly demonstrated to her one night when she was returning from an astral projection she had undertaken in an effort to find him after he disappeared one weekend.

She was returning from her astral journey just as he came into their home. Still in her astral body, she floated above their living room, watching as he came in followed by a being she described as looking like a dark cloud with hands and eyes. Extending from the center of the being was a dark rope which, like a perverted umbilical cord, flowed from the being into the root chakra of her husband.

Her first instinct was to do battle with the creature in order to detach it from her husband, but as she started to attack, it turned to her and "spoke" (most beings who are native to the astral plane do not speak as we know speech, but communicate mentally in images that we translate as words). It told her that her husband was not hers anymore, so not to bother trying to get rid of it (the creature). She ignored the warning and, with the assistance of her guide, was able to get rid of the being temporarily, but since it had been invited to attach itself to her husband by his own actions, she could not keep it away permanently.

Another way to make sure you return from each astral adventure untouched by harmful beings is to pause just before you "reenter" yourself and mentally take a critical look at either your astral body or at the aura of light-energy surrounding your physical body.

If there has been an attempt by any negative astral being to attach itself to your energy field, you will see the evidence on one or both of your etheric bodies in the form of dark patches or strings connecting to your chakra points. These indicate that a negative being has either attempted to attach itself to you or that it has already done so, and is using you as a source of energy the way a vampire seeks a source of fresh blood.

These attachments can be dealt with in a variety of ways (outlined below). Experimentation will quickly clarify which works best for you.

Methods of Detaching Negative Astral Beings

1. Use an astral blade, culled from your imagination, to sever the attachments and discard them into the womb of Mother Earth.

2. Mentally create a purifying fire that you will pass through to cleanse yourself and remove astral debris.

3. Do a full-blown chakra cleansing and balancing as described in the previous chapter.

4. Mentally create an astral shower of golden-white light energy to wash over and through you, removing the attachment and rebalancing your emotional self.

5. Sink your astral body deep into the earth below you, effectively grounding all negative energy attached to you; when you rise from the ground, you will be cleansed.

6. Ask your spirit guide (see next section) to remove them, or to show you how best to deal with them in the future.

The Important Role of Spirit Guides

You can also call on your spirit guides for assistance. These are benevolent, highly evolved beings whose job it is to assist you through life's journey, though you may either not know they exist or not have consciously met them yet. Some feel these guides are the guardian angels people often speak about when they have been rescued miraculously from a dangerous situation by a spiritual hand. Almost everyone who astral projects or meditates regularly is aware of at least one such guide, though usually there is more than one attached to each person. Apparently we humans are a real handful, and it takes more than one guide to get us through our lives.

Your spirit guides are your soul's personal guardians and teachers, and they can be interacted with face to face on the astral plane. They will also help protect you while you travel in the astral world and guide you toward the places you need to go and things you need to see in order to advance spiritually.

It is advisable to facilitate a meeting with your principal guide early in your astral projection experiments. To do this, you will simply go into as deep an altered state of consciousness as possible, and mentally call out to him or her to meet you just after you are successfully projected. A being should appear to you almost immediately in a form that is pleasing. The being may even be vaguely familiar to you; it should assist you in making your leap onto the astral plane.

Since so many of our altered state experiences have a surrealistic quality to them, it can sometimes be difficult to realize that the events are real and so are the beings we meet there. It's easy at first to discount the guide who appears to you as being no more than a product of your imagination. One of the best ways to tell real from unreal—if there is such a distinction—is to gauge your emotional state. Most first meetings with spirit guides are highly emotional. The high vibrational levels and powers of unconditional love are things that most of us never experience until that first meeting, and the feelings they engender can be overwhelming. Physical contact with the guide (hugs, touches, etc.) will intensify these emotions.

My principal spirit guide first appeared to me in an androgynous form while I was in deep meditation. My goal was to astral project to a time and place where I could find the root cause of an ongoing physical problem. It took me several minutes to realize that the figure was a feminine one, in loose robes of a kind that I can't say I'd ever seen before.

She was very focused on me, something that's jarring after living in a world where self-involvement is the norm. She allowed me to lead the progress of our sessions and never forced me to view anything or go anywhere that I did not want to go, even when it would have been for the best for me to do so. I had to make all the decisions about where I was going and what I wanted, then she would show me the best way. She was (and still is) infinitely patient, and exudes a great deal of love. Holding back tears of joy in her presence is not easy.

If the being who appears to you is not in a pleasing form or if he or she makes you feel uncomfortable, then you may be in the presence of a lower astral entity who is playing games. If you feel the need, test the being who appears. The being will not be offended if he or she is truly your principal guide. Ask questions of it about your spiritual life that only your personal spirit guide would know, and ask to be told things that make you sure of its origins and intentions. These include questions about your faith and your journey to find personal truth. Vacillation, badgering, and name calling on the part of the entity, or attempts to coerce you to do something you don't want to, are a sure sign to retreat quickly.

If you are still unsure at all about the being who claims to be your guide, remember that you do not have to go off with this being on its say-so any more than you would go off with someone you just met in the physical world. Take your time. Get to know this being before traveling with it any deeper into the astral plane.

No one agrees on just how the concept of spirit guides originated or how they are selected for their roles, but most agree that they perform their tasks very well. When there is a breakdown in the relationship, it is we humans who are usually at fault. As with our deities, we find it easy to ignore our guides until we're in need and are thus compelled to seek their guidance, forgetting that if we would have just worked with them all along we might not have gotten into such bad shape in the first place. I'm as guilty on this score as anyone, and I'm very thankful that the nature of spirit guides is one of patience, infinite love, and forgiveness.

One of the greatest things a spirit guide can do for us is to guide us through that great compendium of universal knowledge known as the Akashic Records (see chapter 11 for a complete look at this concept). A spirit guide can show you where to look for answers to specific spiritual or karmic questions, where to find the secrets of your soul's past, and how to interpret what you find so that you can use it to improve your current life. Unlocking this knowledge is the reason most people want to astral project in the first place, and your spirit guide can be an invaluable advisor.

Once you get to know your principal spirit guide, you will find the relationship to be one of the most fulfilling of your existence. Your guide can teach you, protect you, offer insights as you explore the astral world, and introduce you to your other guides and teachers—beings who can assist you in making wise decisions about all of your life's issues.

The Lower Astral Levels

Some astral travelers believe that it is possible to suddenly fall into the lower astral realms as easily as you might tumble through a trap door in your floor, even though you've so far been sailing along unharmed in the higher reaches of that plane. It may be possible for this to happen if you suddenly decide to act on less than positive thoughts, but most of the time you will remain safely on the higher side of the border between the lower and higher astral worlds.

Remember that these are not space designations, but vibrational ones. The lower and higher astral worlds overlap and interpenetrate with one another in much the same way as the astral world overlaps and interpenetrates our own. Even though it is there all the time, jumping from one to the other is not easy.

There is a bleed between the higher and lower planes, creating places where the separation between the two is thin. It is true that, in these places, lower beings can reach you—even though you are actually not directly within the lower astral regions. However, this really does not happen as often as astral folklore might suggest.

Because the atmosphere in the lower astral plane is noticeably denser than in the higher, some people say that a sudden heavy sensation is an indication that you may be encountering a questionable area, even when there is no other supporting evidence that you are in the lower regions. After speaking with lots of astral travelers and experiencing the sensation myself, I can safely say that this is usually only a carryover sensation from your physical existence, and most often is not a sign that you've floated into a trouble spot.

In the cycles of REM or dream sleep, which is the same state you are in while astral projecting (see chapter 10), the physical body is paralyzed as a defense mechanism to keep you from leaping out of bed and acting out your dreams. I believe that this sensation is sometimes passed on into the consciousness of the astral body and creates a feeling of heaviness. If this happens to you, try mentally willing your astral self to be light and free. It should happen immediately. If it doesn't, then it is best to return to your body and try again later, when your mindset is such that you can easily remain in the higher levels of the astral plane.

Another occurrence that is rare, but can be disturbing, is hearing human voices calling for help from the lower astral world. Sometimes these are the spirits of deceased humans who have stumbled into these realms because of a belief that this is where they belonged after death. For these beings, it is a hell of their own making from which only time and knowledge can save them. Some tribal shamans have been able to rescue these souls, but it is not a good idea for the novice to try. This is a specialized practice that requires expert control of the astral environment.

There is also the possibility that these voices are coming from lower astral beings who only want to distract or entrap you. If you hear these pleas for help, tell your guides and allow them to deal with the problem.

Fear of Harm to the Physical Body

Astral projection is sometimes defined as the separation of the soul from its physical shell, a much too simplistic explanation that is largely out of favor among modern occultists. Several very old occult schools of thought teach that each living human being has four distinct bodies: the physical body, the astral or emotional body, the mental body, and the spiritual or soul body. They are roughly conceptualized as interpenetrating and overlapping, with the lightest, more spiritually evolved bodies dominating the upper half of the body.

When you project your astral body, or your emotional consciousness, you leave behind not just the physical shell but the mental body (the analytical, intellectual aspect) and the spiritual body (what we think of as the soul or animating life force, which is most easily able to reach the realm of the divine).

These mental and spiritual bodies do not cease to function while your astral self is exploring elsewhere; they remain functioning and are able to offer both physical and psychic protection to your inert body. They are also the media through which you retain a thread of awareness of your physical self while you are projecting and that allows you to be instantly alert should an emergency arise that requires your full attention. Even with these other two bodies on guard for you, many people

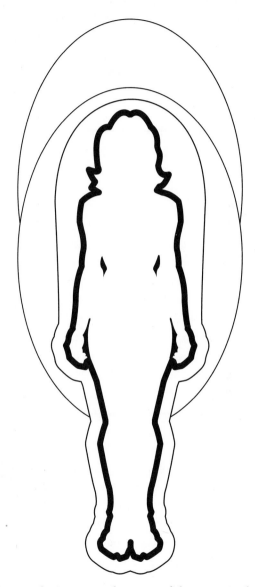

Figure 4. Conceptualization of the Four Bodies

like to give their physical bodies some other means of protection from both physical dangers and psychic attack.

One of the best ways to protect your physical self is by employing the same method you use to help protect your astral self from attracting harmful energies: by ridding yourself of negative thoughts and feelings before attempting to project. Visualize them breaking up and fading away from your physical self somewhere between your meditation and your actual astral projection.

Two other good ways are to make sure your work area is private and that you will not be disturbed, and that you keep your efforts private. Not permitting intruders to come into the room where your sleeping body lies is common sense. The unexpected noises they would make would be startling and would probably result in what we call the *snap back*, where the astral body rejoins the other bodies instantaneously rather than assimilating slowly, as is preferred. This condition is not harmful, but it is very unpleasant and similar to the sensation of being awakened suddenly from a deep sleep or a bad dream. There is about as much chance of a human intruder causing you bodily harm while astral projecting as there is when you're sleeping. Chances are if someone means to harm you, your mental body will bring you to full waking consciousness as soon as it senses danger.

The mental body is sometimes thought to be synonymous with the human aura, the misty egg of colored light that surrounds all living things. The aura has been seen by those trained to view it, and can be photographed with special equipment. It is a barometer of both the physical and mental state; its color and condition is indicative of personality, health, and emotional state. When you mentally strengthen this force before projecting, you increase its efficiency in your defense.

Other things you can do to feel secure while projecting are to surround yourself with another kind of protective egg, one of impenetrable, high vibrational energy. This is a very old practice, one commonly taught to students of deep meditation as well. As you relax your body and prepare to alter your consciousness, simply visualize this egg in place around you. You may want to see it being placed there by a deity or spirit guide, or you can mentally visualize it being drawn up from the loving energy of the earth beneath you or streaming down from the heavens above. If you need to color your energy to make it real for you, try using white or gold, which are traditional colors of protection in several occult circles. This auric egg will not be visible to any human eye unless that person is highly psychic, but it will be real on the astral and you will be able to see it in place if you project out into the room in which you are lying. The more you visualize it being in place, the stronger it will become.

You may also want to have with you on your physical body some item that symbolizes protection, such as a piece of religious jewelry, a holy book, an amulet or talisman, or symbol of deity. No one works better than any other. The efficacy of the item you choose depends solely on how strongly you feel about it as a source of protective energy.

Occasionally, one hears stories about people who have met with accidents while astral projecting and, when they awaken, their physical bodies bear evidence of the astral encounter. Such tales are rare, and I have not seen any documentation on them, but I believe they are a creation of the mind. Your astral body cannot be hurt in the same ways that your physical body can. Your astral self can carry back to your physical body emotional scars or string-like attachments from negative beings, both of which can affect your physical self over time, but it cannot, for example, be hit by a car and leave your physical self wounded—unless you so strongly believe in the possibility that it becomes true.

If you doubt that the mind is powerful enough to accomplish this, then you are not going to be as successful at astral projection (or any other occult endeavor) as you'd like. Most people who are deeply into alternative spirituality or New Age philosophy of any kind are already aware that the mind can heal or inflict illness. Often this knowledge is no more than an intellectual awareness; the student fails to realize that the link between mind and body is made stronger in the astral realm by the emotional connection forged between them by the astral self. If you are hit by a car in the astral and you sincerely believe that your body is hurt, it will be. Rest assured that most of us will never have these problems. It is much more likely that you will be fully aware of your astral self as a spirit body rather than a physical one and, like most newcomers, will delight in watching physical things pass through you as if you weren't really there.

If you are "injured" in the astral, simply remove yourself from the scene of the accident and remind yourself that you are in a spirit form and that your physical self is far away and safe. Spend a few moments visualizing your astral self being healed of all injuries and becoming pure and whole again. Tell yourself that as you do this any wounds on your physical body are also being healed, and that you will return to a healthy, safe body when your astral journey is complete.

Fear of Becoming Lost or Being Unable to Return

Occasionally someone will have an astral projection experience in which the feeling arises that something is blocking the path back to the physical body; or, there might be a sensation of being lost in the astral world, unable to find one's way home again. These occurrences are relatively rare when compared to the number of successful projections. The horror stories they've generated have made a lot of people fearful of astral projection.

Any altered state of consciousness, including the one you will experience during astral projection, shares similarities with clinical hypnosis. Basically, you are seeking to heighten and focus your awareness to the exclusion of other distractions. But even if you are normally what is called a *deep level subject* in hypnosis (that is, someone who finds it difficult to awaken from this state without help), your astral projection consciousness will remain fully under your control. As an added safeguard, you may wish to condition yourself with an astral *automatic return button*. This is a word or phrase that will automatically trigger you to wake yourself when it's employed. As with the protective egg, the more you use it, the stronger it will be become. I like to use the phrase "I am home" as my return button. The simple act of thinking or astrally saying these words immediately awakens me.

To set up your own automatic return button, simply come up with a trigger word or phrase, and tell yourself several times that that particular word or phrase will instantly awaken you. Keep the phrase short, positive, and in the present tense. Present-tense affirmations are standard occult practice. This convinces your mind that the thing you desire is already happening—that it is part of your current reality. Phrasing sentences in the future tense may keep them in your future, always just out of reach. For example, when you need to return to your awakened state quickly, you don't want to say, "I will go home." Your subconscious may just respond with, "OK, sure. When?" and keep you right where you are until you clear up the confusion.

This automatic return programming is best done just after you are comfortably in an altered state of consciousness, but before you attempt to astral project. Spend several minutes focusing on this verbal image. Allow yourself to mentally see these words so that their intended function can be impressed on both your conscious and subconscious minds.

This automatic return button should only be used in situations when you feel afraid or sense that you are unable to return to your normal consciousness any other way. Under most circumstances you will exit your projections by the same method you used to enter them. This is another of those long-accepted occult practices. Not only is it a smooth and gentle way to awaken, but when you undo something in the precise reverse order of the way you did it, you rob your conscious critical mind of the power to tell you that what you're doing doesn't make sense to it. That way, it cannot interfere in your practice. For instance, if you exit your body from your crown chakra, that's the route by which you would return; if you follow a rainbow path or a cave trail into the astral world, you would follow it back out again.

Keeping track of all clear landmarks and visual points you find along the pathway both in and out of your astral travels can provide guideposts for getting home. If you ever start to feel lost, just turn your astral self around and begin to retrace your steps.

Another quick way out is by willing yourself to be home again. At the risk of sounding repetitive, never forget that thought is action on the astral plane. Willing yourself to be somewhere else is the easiest mode of travel. Do this by shifting your focus immediately from your astral experience to your body. Once you imagine your consciousness back in your body and get a sense of the physical you, you can open your eyes.

You can also ask your guide to help you get home if you lose track of landmarks or find that the act of willing yourself home is being blocked. Be aware that these blocks usually come from fears living within our own psyches rather than from any sinister denizen of the astral world. They occasionally happen, and our guides are well equipped to help us overcome them. The guide usually helps you retrace your steps and gives you the confidence you need to reenter your waking consciousness.

Some people say they are aware of a silver cord, or luminescent etheric rope, connecting their physical bodies to their astral ones. If you are one of those who see this, you can simply gather up your cord and follow it home should you feel lost. Much folklore surrounds this cord, which is reputed to connect body and soul. Many believe that if the cord is damaged or severed, the soul will be released from the body and the body will die. I have never seen this cord, nor do I personally know anyone who has, though I have read countless accounts depicting it.

Over time I have been of two minds about the nature of this mysterious life line. One is that it is a construct of the subconscious, a sort of mental security blanket to hold onto while traveling in the unknown. The other is that the cord may be indicative of a different sort of projection where the mental body or parts of the spiritual body are involved. But since a great many people never see this cord or worry about its condition, it should not be one of the fears that holds you back.

A few people worry about what the sight of their physical bodies will do to them when viewed from an outside perspective. They fear that when they see their own bodies from the outside, they may panic, flee, and get lost with no way to return.

Having experienced astral projection in a variety of settings, I can say with certainty that this is not a frightening event but rather one that, for many of us, validates the astral experience. Granted, it is an odd sensation; it might be upsetting or startling to someone who knows nothing of astral projection and might fear they have just died. But for those of us who are informed, this is not a problem. Just the opposite—it can be fascinating to watch your sleeping body from outside its confines.

Fear Purging and Mind Conditioning

By this point, it should be clear to you that one of the greatest impediments to success in any occult endeavor are one's own fear and hang-ups. Because of this, I strongly recommend what I call purging sessions, followed in most cases by some simple mind conditioning exercises to eliminate these blockages before they can hinder your progress.

To begin, make a few notes in your astral journal about the things you most fear about the process. This can be anything from the common fears already mentioned to your own deepest horror. Try to go beyond the first thoughts that come into your mind and really delve into your psyche. It's not easy for most of us to admit our fears, least of all to write them out word for frightening word.

Keeping your fears in mind, go to the place where you will be projecting and lie down or sit comfortably. Take a few deep breaths and relax. At this point there is no need to take yourself into an altered state, though you may find yourself drifting in this direction during this exercise.

Next, imagine that you are projected and are drifting free on the astral plane. See each detail clearly as if it was the pilot for a television show playing in your head. When you are comfortable with your inner vision, cue the fear to come into the scene. See yourself interact with it, or flee from it, or turn it to good, or whatever else you think you would do should it appear.

You should be aware that this is not the type of visualization that is going to draw these mental images into your life. Just the opposite—by dealing with them now in a non-projected state but with your full imagination engaged in the process, you are working through your fears and banishing them from all levels of your being. When you cease to have fear, you release the magnetic energy that attracts it to you. In short, by dealing with it before you astral project, you accomplish two things:

1. You show your conscious mind, that critic who always tries to keep you from doing things, that you can handle these situations, and

2. You release the fear from your subconscious where it lies waiting to pounce on you when you least expect it.

When you are finished dealing with each fear or blockage, finish killing it off by mentally seeing it dissipate. You can do this in several ways. You can see it fade away and vanish; mentally draw an *X* through it; allow it to sink harmlessly into the earth; explode, etc.— whatever impresses the fact on your subconscious that this problem no longer exists. Once you have accomplished this, take a few more deep breaths and allow your mind to release these visions.

You should also spend some time "practice projecting," a process that conditions your mind to view the world from other points of view. This is the way you will most likely view the astral plane once you've projected, but it can be disconcerting the first time it happens. Some people even find it disturbing or dream-like, and are unsure that their projections are legitimate.

Keeping your eyes closed, mentally select a few inanimate objects around the room you are in and, one by one, pretend that your consciousness has just leaped from your body into that object. Using both your imagination and your mental eyes, try to view your surroundings from the point of view of this stationary object. It's best to select objects that will give you a variety of different viewpoints for comparison.

Try to memorize what you see and, when you open your eyes again, go stand at the site of these objects and look around to see just how well you were able to imagine what the room looked like from their angle. While it will be largely your imagination at work, your subconscious will start to be conditioned to being in a projected state and, if you slipped into an altered state while doing this experience, you may even confirm some things you saw that will tell you that you were actually, if only for a moment, astrally projected.

Summary Statements

Back in the early days of the Great Depression, American president Franklin Delano Roosevelt summed up the paralyzing nature of fear best when he announced to the world that we have "nothing to fear but fear itself." Fear renders us immobile, unable to act or think clearly. It clouds our judgment and confuses our efforts, and it makes us vulnerable to those who prey on weaknesses. Worst of all, it keeps us from having the courage to strive for our goals.

Courage is not the absence of fear, but rather the determination to forge ahead in the face of fear and to overcome it. It is the spirit of perseverance. As you continue to practice astral projection, you will come to realize you are fully capable of dealing with any emergency in both the physical or astral world, and your fears will fade. Have courage!

CHAPTER 4

Keys to Success

There are several methods you can use to achieve astral projection, and some techniques will work better for you than others. Though you will find a great many similarities in methods, most people find astral projecting to be a very individual art, and you will soon discover that certain aspects must be tailored to suit your needs. The best route to success is to experiment until you find the one or ones that resonate with your inner self, allowing you to slip easily onto the astral plane. As you read through the detailed instructions of the various astral projection methods in the following six chapters, you may get an instant sense of this resonance. Conversely, you may need to experiment with all of the techniques to find the one(s) most suited to you.

The First Key: Focus

To be fair to the method you've chosen initially, promise yourself to give it at least a month before moving on to others. Some people learn to project successfully within a few weeks, others will take a few years. Don't let the time involved discourage you. Anything worthwhile takes time, and your efforts will be rewarded. I know of no one who has not eventually succeeded at astral projection whenever honest and consistent effort has been made. Three other tips can help keep you successfully focused on the goal:

1. Know and control your state of mind.

2. Take immediate control of your direction.

3. Keep your emotional involvement strong.

Know and Control Your State of Mind

The controversial occultist Aleister Crowley (1875–1947) coined the term *will-less will*, meaning the state of mind required for successful occult operations. I've always thought it a perfect description. In one respect, you need to remain focused on your goal (the will), but at the same time straining to keep that focus will only set up tensions in your body and mind that will hamper you, so you also need to achieve a certain sense of detachment from your effort (the will-less).

While this sounds easy in principle, I've found that this was one of the hardest states of mind to learn to achieve. In my case I wanted to astral project so badly that, when it finally happened, I became so excited I ended up right back inside myself, starting all over again. It wasn't until I let go of the desperation and just let it happen with a will-less will that I was able to control the process.

When you realize for the first time that you're successful—or are about to be—try as much as possible to maintain a casual attitude about it, as if your success was expected and no less than you deserve.

Take Immediate Control of Your Direction

When you first think that you've successfully astral projected, you shouldn't be afraid to participate in the creation of your astral world. Rather than risk a quick return to your body, you should immediately begin to form the scenes that you wish to see in your mind. Allow your astral self to be there. Don't worry that you are fooling yourself or making everything up as you go along. The astral world is as fluid as thought. Give it a gentle push and trust it to meet you halfway.

The best way to maintain your position within the astral plane is to engage your mind in a scene or event with which you can become emotionally involved—this is where those inner fantasy exercises from chapter 2 can pay off. Once you become emotionally involved with a scene while in a projected state, you will find that you've given yourself a launching pad in the astral plane from which you can travel anywhere, or to any time.

Keep Your Emotional Involvement Strong

When you are first released from the confines of your physical consciousness, it's best to immediately transfer your consciousness elsewhere. This can be into another astral vehicle or into another place or time, just so long as it's somewhere important to you. Too many beginners are taught to simply lift an astral double out from their physical body and allow it to float around the room, looking back down at itself. Both your subconscious and conscious minds are likely to ask you, "What's the point?" For a few astral travelers this vision is comforting and therefore emotionally involving, but for most of us it seems to get in the way of progress.

Remember that the astral body is also called the *emotional body*. This connection cannot be over-stressed. The more your emotions are involved in your astral projection efforts, the easier those efforts will be. Viewing the room where your body lies can be difficult because there is little emotional connection going on unless you harbor deep fears about leaving it behind. It is much better, and usually easier, to find a place in the astral realm where your entire being can find interest and excitement and you will have little trouble keeping your consciousness focused there.

The Second Key: Gaining Confidence by Gauging Success

Beginners often get frustrated with their early astral projection efforts because, while they know something different is happening to them, they are not sure if they are being successful or not. Unfortunately there is no way anyone else can give you a definitive answer to that question. However, there are nine checkpoints that may help you decide for yourself.

First Checkpoint:
Note Any Sensations after "Leaving" the Body

Be prepared for, and aware of, unusual sights, sounds, or sensations experienced as your astral and physical selves begin to separate. Whether or not you're aware of it, you've probably had similar experiences if you've ever endured physical trauma or severe pain. Think about how you seemed to be slightly detached from yourself at the time; how the memories seem hazy, as though you're looking through a cloud, and how all the sights and sounds around you at the time seemed distant and vague. Do you remember the point at which you began to feel better, and suddenly everything seemed to appear clearer to you? It may be that the haze was caused by your astral (emotional) self peering back at your body through astral space while it sought a safe place to hide until the ordeal was over.

Three phenomena, either appearing individually or together, seem to be present in most successful projections: swaying sensations, lights, and sounds.

Swaying Sensations. The first phenomenon, which is often experienced at the threshold of astral projection, is a sensation of motion. This will often occur even if the projection is not fully successful. Between the time it takes to reach the deepest level of altered state that you are going to achieve and the moment of actually projecting your astral body, many practitioners report experiencing a swaying feeling. This is similar to being bobbed about in a rowboat, but without the attendant nausea. Some people feel that this sensation is literally the astral double separating from its physical shell.

A tip for helping you make the final separation from your physical consciousness is to just flow with the feeling without trying to force yourself any further. I've always enjoyed the sensation and find it pleasant to ride it out to its conclusion. If you can allow yourself to feel engulfed in the gentle rocking sensation without trying to direct it, you'll often find that separation will occur on its own shortly afterward.

Lights. The second phenomenon is the sighting of small colored lights as the astral plane is first entered. Many occult writings refer to these "astral lights," but few attempt to define what they might be. I've always felt they were a creation of the mind as it enters a deeper altered state of consciousness, similar to lights that can sometimes be seen flashing behind the eyelids as you first enter sleep. Suffice it to say that these lights are usually an indication that you have successfully passed into another plane of consciousness.

Sounds. The third phenomenon, that of sound, is the rarest of the three, but still occurs often enough that you need to be aware of its existence. Just before or after full separation of the astral body, many astral travelers report hearing a buzzing sound similar to that of a swarm of insects on a hot summer night. Sometimes the buzzing takes on a musical, if atonal, aspect, and may sound like a chorus of disembodied voices humming in disharmony. The first time I heard these noises they sounded as if they were being whispered directly into my ear. I was unprepared for them, and ended up being startled out of my altered state.

Explanations for the origin of these astral sounds are legion. They have been credited to stresses in the astral atmosphere where it has opened to admit you; to astral-dwelling faeries, also called nature spirits; to spirits who hover near the borders of the two worlds, perhaps protecting these boundaries; and to discarnate humans, spirits of the deceased, trying to get the attention of astral travelers who still have physical bodies. The "faces" behind the sounds have never shown themselves to anyone of my acquaintance, nor have they ever harmed anyone to my knowledge, so take their presence simply as a sign that you have successfully astral projected, and don't allow them to distract you from your altered state.

Second Checkpoint:
Compare Your Experience to the Definition

You are astral projected *anytime your consciousness is immersed in another time and/or place from that of your physical body.* Even if you retain some awareness of your physical self while projecting, that does not mean your astral self and all that it is experiencing in the astral world is not equally real. The acceptance that both the astral world and the physical world are both real places, that they exist simultaneously, and that there are now two aspects of the true you, each in a different place and having a different experience, is hard for many beginners to understand. The process of dual acceptance can be further undermined by the fact that you will often remain aware of your physical body and its surroundings while you are in the astral world.

I was once deeply involved in an astral projection in which my spirit guide was showing me answers to a particularly plaguing issue. While she was doing this, I was fully aware that there were tears flowing from my physical body, but this in no way detracted from the clarity of the astral vision. I accepted both worlds as real, and the reactions of both my beings to the events unfolding were proper. I also had no doubt that I was astral projecting at the time.

Also, don't assume failure if your projections have dream-like qualities. Dreams are no more than uncontrolled astral projections and, like dreams, astral projections can seem very surreal. Part of this is caused by the "thought is action" aspect of the astral plane. Another way dreams and astral projections compare is that the clarity of both tend to fade after awakening unless the experience is recorded in detail. Beginners will find this fading of astral images more of a problem than advanced astral travelers. Beginners are also more likely to question the validity of their experiences later on, so good record keeping is essential.

Take comfort in the fact that, with experience, your astral projections will grow more vivid and more memorable, and it will become easier to put them into perspective once you awaken from them. In time you may even learn to categorize projections by their clarity, quality, how memorable they are, and other characteristics. I have a hierarchy of astral projection qualities that I use to rate my experiences. I do this immediately upon completing an astral journey, while my impression of its overall character is still fresh.

Sometimes, no matter how well we aim for a certain kind of astral projection (for instance, going to a specific place or time), the astral self has its own ideas about what it wants to do. As long as you are able to control some aspect of the experience, it is probably a valid astral journey. In this scenario, I try to look at all aspects of the experience, and then attempt to plug it into one of four broad categories:

1. Spirit contact is initiated by a deceased relative or friend.
2. Other astral world beings are initiating contact.
3. A spontaneous past-life regression happens.
4. A spirit guide is controlling the projection in order to teach me something.

Third Checkpoint: Take Note of Your Astral Projection Point of View

If you are astral projecting and are able to view your surroundings from unique perspectives, such as from the astral self's eyes or from high above the scene, these are good signs of success. Being able to view your projections from the point of view of the astral body without forcing the perspective is an excellent sign that you are really astral projecting.

Occultists used to teach that this latter perspective—the distant one, which is also called the broad or remote view—was an indication that you were *not* projecting successfully, but myself and many other people have viewed our projections in this manner too often to discount them. I think a lot of this shift in perspective has to do with the influence of television and the movies; we are obviously quite used to following the main character (the point of view character) from outside of that character's body. We watch from a distance, seeing the main character (whose thoughts and feelings we adopt) only from the outside. In this way we have learned to identify with characters without occupying the same physical space. Keep in mind that your emotional involvement in the vision you are beholding is a much more accurate barometer than mere point of view.

Also, take note of any scene you see from simultaneous multiple points of view. This phenomenon is called *omniscient sight*, and it can literally give you eyes in the back of your head. You may suddenly realize that you can see in a complete 360-degree circle, or that you are simultaneously viewing the world from two completely opposing places, such as from your own astral body and from the eyes of someone else who is present. These are excellent indicators that you are astral projecting. If you find these points of view disturbing, either mentally will them away or try the old occultist's trick of covering the set of eyes you don't want with a hood, hat, or other piece of clothing.

Fourth Checkpoint:
Check for the Phenomenon of Time Distortion

Current occult thought seems to be leaning toward a theory that everything you see or experience on the astral plane is actually taking place simultaneously, but is only experienced sequentially by your conscious mind. This would correspond to our current knowledge about the nature of time, as well as with findings in many dream and memory studies.

Time does not exist outside of our physical world—just ask any physicist. In the astral world, you experience time as it really is: omnipresent. There is no past and future, only your perception of it, which is why you are able to view past lives through astral projection. On the astral plane things may appear to happen very rapidly or very slowly, though you will be unable to tell which until you awaken. If you find much more or less time has passed than you thought should have gone by while you were projected, then you were likely successful.

Also, if you come back from your astral travels feeling as though you've really been away, and that your surroundings are places you have missed, that is a good sign too. I remember a night that I returned to normal consciousness only to find I'd been gone for five hours. I actually felt as if I'd been traveling. I had that same "glad to be home" feeling you get when you've been away a long time. I was both tired—as any traveler tends to be—and energized.

If you experience time distortions of any kind, no matter how small or how excessive, you can be sure that you are succeeding.

Fifth Checkpoint:
What Can You Control on Your Astral Journeys?

If you find you are able to control yourself more and more, but are less and less able to control or predict the actions of other astral beings, then you are probably successfully projecting. When you first astral project, you will feel like you are controlling everything, making it all up as you go along. As you gain experience and travel deeper into the astral world, you should begin to notice that other beings are reacting to you in the same way physical beings react to your physical self. You will not be able to control them as you would in a daydream or other controlled fantasy. This too is a sign of success.

Sixth Checkpoint:
Be Wary of Trying to Immediately
Verify Your Astral Experiences

Some people like to work with a partner to test the validity of their astral projection experiences, and will astrally travel to each other's home to see what's going on and then have the partner verify the events. This does not always work as well as you might think it should. The aforementioned problem of time distortion makes coordinating events between the physical world with events in the clockless astral realm very difficult.

I tried this type of experiment with a friend when I was first learning to control my projections, and the first scene I happened in upon was so real that I rushed to the phone to describe it in vivid detail to my partner, who sadly informed me that I was completely wrong. I felt defeated and began to doubt myself and my skills until the friend called back several hours later to tell me that the events I had witnessed hours before had just taken place within the past few minutes. There were some glitches. For instance, I had described my friend as brewing a cup of tea when I was actually seeing her hanging over a steaming kettle to ease the symptoms of the head cold she was fighting.

For the most part I was seeing everything accurately, but I was forgetting the time factor. Had the time difference between these two events been more than a few hours, we would both likely have forgotten all about it and never made the connection.

The point is that you can try these experiments, but be cautious about deciding your astral projection efforts have failed just because you don't have immediate physical world verification of your achievement.

Seventh Checkpoint:
Be Wary of Comparing Your Astral Experiences with Others, Regardless of Their Skill Level

Comparing your astral plane experiences to those of your friends is useful only if you seek to learn from them and not hold them up as a standard for yourself. Everyone has a slightly different experience while projecting and a slightly different way in which they perceive their disassociation from their physical bodies.

The friend and working partner I just mentioned has vastly different experiences than me. She tends to stay in the present world around familiar people and places. I, on the other hand, often find myself in the past or in distant places I have never been.

Part of this difference can be attributed to the goals that we each set for our astral projection experiences, as well as our varied interests and personal thought patterns. We also experience the "thought is action" law in different ways. For her it is simply a case of thinking "I wonder what would happen if I did this," and then she will suddenly find herself engaging in the activity. For me it is a matter of thinking about what would happen if a certain action happened to me, and then I find myself automatically doing whatever I need to do in order to cause the action to occur.

She acts and I am more acted on, but both events are initiated by our own thoughts and both are valid astral projections.

Eighth Checkpoint:
Be Wary of Anachronisms and Bleed-throughs from Other Aspects of Yourself

Even in the astral world, you remain the sum of your whole being. Though your astral body may be the one primarily having the experience, you still have a physical self, a mental self, and a soul, all of which bring some measure of themselves into the astral adventure. No matter how fully absorbed you are in the astral world, don't be surprised if you occasionally find oddities of time or place, or an awareness of other lives creeping in (past, present, future), all of which are clearly products of your other selves. Don't let these bother you or allow them to convince you that you are not really astral projecting.

Initially, I had a great deal of difficulty if any anachronisms in the time frame that I had projected into appeared. Even though the overall astral experience was clear and easy to follow, I would let just one tiny glitch upset me to the point where I could not continue. It took lots of experimentation and the intervention of both my guide and other astral projectors to teach me that being hypercritical was only impeding my progress.

Unless anomalies become constant or extremely surreal—which could indicate that you've fallen asleep and are dreaming—simply note them for what they are and consider your astral experience valid.

Ninth Checkpoint:
Looking Out for Number Two

On rare occasions, astral travelers will report sighting a second astral self; that is, a self other than the one into which their consciousness has deliberately been projected. This double is sometimes called by the German term *doppelgänger* or by the Old English appellation *fetch*. Neither term is adequate for explaining what this means in astral terms, since in both Germanic and Anglo-Norman folklore the appearance of these spectral doubles to those still in the physical world was thought to be an omen of one's approaching death.

I have seen my own astral double several times in either the earliest or latest parts of my astral travels, and believe it to be a manifestation of the mental or spiritual self that is outside of, but still connected to, the physical body. It appears only at the beginning and end of projections because, by nature, it must remain closer to the body than the astral self, which has more freedom to travel. This seems to confirm a theory that this other self may simply be extending itself in order to guard the physical self until your astral body returns, and that it is a manifestation present in most altered state exercises, but which is not always solid enough to be seen even with the astral eyes.

If you see a doppelgänger at all, it will likely take you by surprise the first time. I know it did me. With my head full of dark European legends, I immediately felt the unpleasant "snap back" sensation associated with a quick arousal from the altered state. The experience felt just as it does when one awakens from a nightmare:

heavy breathing, reorientation to the waking world, and the relieved assurance that all is well.

If your doppelgänger appears while you're floating on the boundaries of the astral world, trust that no harm has come to you.

Summary Statements

I hope this chapter has taught you not to be too critical of your astral projection efforts. Whenever I've spoken with people trying to learn this art, I often find in their descriptions of frustration many clues that tell me they are actually succeeding on some level. Often they miss these indicators because of misconceptions about what astral projection really is or because they are comparing their experiences to someone else's.

The next section of this book goes into detailed methods of achieving astral projection, and each of these will in some way affect the type of projection you have. If you can be less critical of yourself and remain open to these various possibilities, you may find you are better at astral projection than you thought.

PART TWO

SIX METHODS OF ASTRAL PROJECTION

CHAPTER 5

===

Astral Projection
Method 1: General
Transfer of Consciousness

The whole point of astral projection is to move the consciousness, or our internal point of view, into another place. An obvious concept, right? It ought to be, but you'd be surprised how many people who are trying to learn astral projection fail to put that knowledge to use in their early attempts. Often the idea behind shifting the orientation of one's perspective is understood intellectually but, in the emotional struggle to get out of one's body, the shift concept is often tossed aside in favor of a flow of consciousness technique, sometimes called a *lift-out* technique—a method almost always doomed to fail for reasons that will soon become clear.

General Transfer of Consciousness

The *general transfer of consciousness* method of astral projection is the successful alternative. It is the foundation for the methods that will follow in this book. General transfer of consciousness is both a method in its own right and a stepping stone to other techniques, so even if it fails to capture your imagination on its own, please take the time to understand its concepts as well as its pros and cons. Your understanding of these principles will continue to serve you well as you gain experience on the astral plane.

The transfer of consciousness technique allows us to build a separate vehicle into which we can transfer our astral selves before setting off to explore the astral plane. Although it is similar to the aforementioned lift-out technique, there is one key distinction.

The lift-out method is not one generally taught by experienced occult teachers because it rarely, if ever, works well. The idea behind lift-out is to will the astral self to separate from the physical by *mentally following the astral self's progress* while it floats upward out of the body. What this inevitably does is force the mind to focus on your physical body's center of gravity and on a sequence of conscious events rather than on the astral self and its already completed shift in consciousness.

The general transfer of consciousness method bypasses the difficult areas that focus attention on the physical body, which inevitably cause the projector difficulty.

Instead, attention is directed toward the astral vehicle, placing the focus on the spirit.

Unfortunately, the lift-out method is the technique on which most beginners pin their hopes. I tried the lift-out method when I was first attempting to astral project; when I look back on the experience I remember that the visions in my mind while I was doing this were of the front side of my physical self and not on my astral self. I kept wanting to see my entire astral double lifting out from my body in one flowing effort, so I kept my attention on my body alone rather than on making the shift from my physical body to my astral body.

Even though I must have been aware of this problem on some level, I still fully expected that if I could just will it right, I would feel my astral body make the transition simultaneously from head to toe. Hindsight allows me to see the flaws in this idea, but at the time I wasted many nights and a lot of of energy on something that had very little chance of working.

If you are a beginner who wants to remain close to the security of your physical body as you learn to project—and many do—then the general transfer of consciousness into another vehicle may work best for you. The fact that general transfer of consciousness requires that your destination (the astral vehicle) be initially close to your body can be comforting.

However, this fact is also a drawback, since it means that your desire to project must be exceptionally strong. Otherwise, you may not be able to come up with the level of emotional connection to your destination that is necessary in order to interest the astral self in going there. Stepping outside of your physical shell just to float around and see it lying there is not very exciting for your emotional self, so you may have to give it some mental pep talks to get it jump-started. Despite this single draw-back, the general transfer of consciousness method of astral projection remains very popular and many occultists teach it under a variety of names.

Creating an Astral Vehicle

In order to enter the astral realm, you need an astral body, or *astral vehicle*. This is the vehicle into which your consciousness will be transferred during the method we've just discussed—the general transfer of conscious-ness. It can be referred to as any of the following:

1. Simulacrum.

2. Homunculus.

3. Watcher.

4. Astral Eyes.

5. Elemental.

6. Body of Light.

Before you go into your altered state and prepare to project, you need to spend some time deciding just how you wish to visualize your astral vehicle, which, for the purpose of clarity, we'll refer to in this chapter as a *Body of Light*. Some people prefer to visualize it as an astral double of their own physical bodies—either as an exact replica or an idealized state. Others prefer to see it as a simple sphere of gold or white light. Some clearly envision only their heads, while visualizing the rest of the body as a formless, robed area underneath.

For now it is strongly recommended that you avoid assuming animal shapes or the astral guises of other people, both the living and the dead. These vehicles are certainly possible to attain on the astral plane, though they are often difficult. Skilled occultists and shamans use these techniques frequently, but they present a whole other set of difficulties for which the beginner is probably not prepared.

Taking on an animal body propels us into the realm of shapeshifting, an ancient shaman's art that can drastically alter the consciousness and behaviors of the one who assumes the shape. If the person assuming the shape is not fully in control of the energies she or he takes on, the animal energy will take control and lead the projector into places and situations she or he may not be able to handle.

Assuming the guise of another person is another art occasionally used by the skilled shaman and is popularly known as *invocation*. This vehicle form presents similar problems for the beginner. It can also be a violation of the free will of the person whose guise is borrowed, especially if the goal is to use this guise to avoid blame while performing negative actions on the astral plane.

The concept of, and respect for, free will is the common thread lacing through the major occult schools of thought and through many spiritualities and religions. Each school or faith outlines the retribution to be faced for this transgression, and all are similar in their assertion that the harm done will somehow be revisited upon the perpetrator several times over. For now, stick with the simple Body of Light in your own form or that of a simple sphere.

The Transfer of Consciousness Process

To begin working with this method, go to the private, quiet place where you will be practicing your astral projection. Make whatever preparations you wish: light incense, undress, don a talisman, turn on some gentle music, turn up the heat to keep yourself warm, etc. Get into the body posture you have chosen to work in, be it sitting or lying down, and take a few moments to make sure you are comfortable enough to maintain this position for up to an hour. If not, make changes now. If you make changes later, you may unintentionally slip out of your altered state or break your flow of visualization in a disruptive way.

When you are sure you will be comfortable and warm, close your eyes and take a few deep, slow breaths. As you begin to release physical tension, also release any negative thoughts, feelings, or intentions from your mind. With each breath, feel yourself relaxing and being freed from negative energies of any kind. You may wish to visualize this in some way that has meaning for you (see discussion of progressive relaxation on page 12 for ideas).

Continue to breathe slowly, making sure that every part of your physical self is fully relaxed. As a beginner, you may need to spend ten or twenty minutes focusing on each individual part of the body and willing it specifically to unwind. The techniques used for this "progressive relaxation" are fully explained in chapter 1. Until you are used to the sensation of total relaxation, you may not realize that certain small muscle groups are still tense unless you focus exclusively on them and work on relaxing them. There is no need to rush. Take as long as you need for this.

When you feel you are fully relaxed and are feeling peaceful, begin to use whatever method you have chosen to attain an altered state of consciousness. This can be counting, breathing, using a mantra, etc. Don't worry about how deep into the altered state you are able to go at this point. Astral projection doesn't require an ultra-deep state, and many experienced practitioners swear the lighter levels are the best. Just go where it is most natural for you to go at this time. With time and practice your altered state will come easier and faster, and they will naturally deepen. For now, take as much time as you need.

When you feel that you are where you need to be mentally, you are ready to begin building your Body of Light. You should already have a clear picture of the form you wish it to take. A few feet away from your resting physical body, imagine this Body of Light starting to take shape.

Project into it not only your own mental energy, but also energy that you draw from either the earth beneath you or the sky above. This is an old occult trick. You never deplete your own energy stores when undertaking any occult endeavor, but rely instead on those found in nature—in Mother Earth and the eternal sky above you—to help fashion your desire. To do this, just make a mental connection with the source that you wish to draw from, and then visualize a stream of energy moving from it into the object (such as the Body of Light) that you are charging. Don't concern yourself with "obstructions" like floors and ceilings. The divine energy inherent in creation, which you seek to draw energy from, cannot be impeded by something as comparatively insubstantial as the structural components of your home. However, if these impediments bother you, you can mentally cut a hole or place a tube through which the energy can move. Eventually, you will feel comfortable with the fact that this isn't necessary.

By this point in your efforts, time will have ceased to have any meaning for you; all time references made in the instructions beyond this point are guidelines only. For example, when I use the Body of Light method, I usually take what I think is about five minutes to properly fashion this vehicle. In "real" time I have no idea how long it takes. As a beginner you will probably need anywhere from ten to twenty minutes to fully charge and visualize your astral vehicle.

Once the Body of Light is formed in a manner that is pleasing and comfortable to you, and it feels solid and stable, mentally charge it with its duty. This ancient practice of assigning purpose to the Body of Light is called *words of power.* It is an affirmation that we are taking responsibility for our actions. Whenever we create something in the astral world, we must assume responsibility for it throughout the duration of its existence. Additionally, we must dismantle it when its purpose has been served.

Allowing your creation to run loose until it dies on its own from lack of energy to feed on will do one of two things. It could follow you around, making noise or creating "thick" spots in the air, giving you a feeling of being haunted. Or, without your guidance, it could run amok on the astral plane, creating problems for other astral travelers or for your own astral body. This is irresponsible and rude to other astral travelers and to those beings who live on the astral plane. It's the same as someone dropping their child off at your house without notice, then not picking him up again for months.

Tell your Body of Light what it is to do for you by carefully choosing your words and then mentally directing them to the Body of Light. Make these instructions simple and clear. Don't be tempted to use flowery language—it can be misinterpreted—and be sure to back up your words with clear visualizations of what you expect. Clear thoughts such as those found in visualizations mean you are using symbolic language, and this is the language best understood on the astral plane. In this instance the assignment for the Body of Light would be to provide a vehicle for astral exploration, after which it would return safely to your starting place.

You are now ready to transfer your consciousness into this Body of Light, which is where your mind conditioning exercises (chapter 3) are useful. Shift your perception from your physical body into the Body of Light. Don't try to follow it out of your body step by step like in the always fallible lift-out method. This can only lead to an over-emphasis on the body and not on the astral consciousness. As you feel your consciousness is getting the idea of being elsewhere, allow it to shift itself into the Body of Light. Once you are able to see your surroundings from the Body of Light's perspective, you will know you are successful.

It may take several attempts before you can sustain this sensation of your consciousness being somewhere else. Test your transfer of consciousness by looking out at your surroundings every few minutes to see from whose point of view they are being seen, your physical body's or the Body of Light's. If this is your first attempt at projecting, you may not be able to hold your consciousness in the Body of Light for long. Don't let this frustrate you. Just keep practicing getting your consciousness shifted into the Body of Light and keeping it there for as long as possible.

At first, don't try to move away from the spot where your Body of Light has been formed. Just allow your consciousness to look around the immediate area from a stationary position. Until you are used to having your consciousness elsewhere, moving it around will likely only send you right back to yourself and you'll have to begin all over again.

But also remember that you are no longer constrained by the limitations of your physical body, and your eyes can swivel around a full 360-degrees to see everything surrounding you without moving your "head" at all—this is the omniscient sight phenomenon mentioned in chapter 4. Sometimes astral projectors will find they view the world this way no matter where they look. Some people find it exciting and liberating, but for others it is disconcerting. If you find this uncomfortable, merely will a hood or hat to be drawn over the back of your mental eyes and this should put a stop to omniscient sight.

Once you are able to maintain your consciousness within the Body of Light, you can attempt to will it elsewhere. You do not have to methodically follow it out of the area by seeing it move through the ceiling and out over your neighborhood, etc., though you can do this if you like. Simply will yourself to be wherever it is that you want to travel, and you should immediately be taken there by your astral vehicle. Don't worry about slipping out of the Body of Light at some distant location. If your consciousness leaves the Body of Light, it will immediately be back in your physical self.

When you are finished exploring and are ready to quit, mentally will yourself to be back in the same space in which you created the Body of Light. Once there, allow your consciousness to return to your physical self. Mentally willing it there is usually all it takes. You can also simply start "viewing" your surroundings from your physical self's point of view, and that too will work.

You should now dismantle the Body of Light by visualizing it dissipating and sinking harmlessly into the ground beneath you. In many occult schools, the earth has long been used as a tool for grounding unwanted or excess energies. Some practitioners like to see the Body of Light being reabsorbed into their own physical bodies. The reasoning behind this has to do with retaining full levels of personal energy and gaining clearer memory of the astral experience. If you want to experiment to see if this works for you, please do. The method is less important than the end result. What *is* important here is that you take the time to fully dismantle what you've created.

When the Body of Light is gone, begin to regain an awareness of your physical self. Mentally acknowledge the existence of your head and neck, your chest and stomach, and work your way down to your feet. Once you are aware of all these parts, begin to flex your hands and feet and slowly open your eyes.

The last step in this returning process is to seal the portal you have created between the physical and astral worlds by doing something to celebrate your corporeal self. Make noise, eat, have safe sex, or do anything else that affirms your physical existence. If you wish, you can touch the ground or visualize excess energy fading away from yourself. You may think that being projected will be a tiring experience, but you will actually be energized by the process and may find it hard to settle down for several hours afterward. For this reason, the grounding of excess energy is important.

Don't forget to record your experiences, successes, failures, and other impressions in your magical journal or occult diary for later reference.

Opening Your Astral Eyes

A variation on this transfer of consciousness method is a practice known as sending out the *Astral Eyes* or the *Watcher*. This allows you to gather psychic impressions via your astral self that you can assimilate and analyze at a later time without actually having to make a shift in your consciousness. In other words, even if you are having trouble fully astral projecting, this option for gathering remote information is still open to you.

This variation tempts many to use it to spy on others. It must always be remembered that just because it is temporarily separated from us, it is not a separate being. The Astral Eyes are an extension of our selves and we are responsible for their whereabouts. If you send the Astral Eyes out with negative intentions, one of the three following events—or all three—will occur:

1. You will be turned back by the guides and spirit guardians of the person you are spying on.

2. You will be given impressions that are false, disturbing, or that will cause you to act inappropriately based on misleading information.

3. You will be invaded in turn by other astral
   beings wishing to spy on you or otherwise
   violate your free will.

To begin experimenting with your Astral Eyes, follow
all the steps above for forming the Body of Light. You
may want to alter your visualization slightly and allow
the astral vehicle to form as a camera lens or large eye
rather than as a sphere of light. Then, instead of shifting
your consciousness into it, mentally attach it to your
third eye chakra by visualizing a long, elastic rope linking them. Refer to Figure 3 on page 31 if you've forgotten where the seven major chakras are located.

The third eye chakra is the one most often associated
with psychic skills, and makes the perfect receptacle for
any astral impressions that your Astral Eyes gather. In clear
and precise language or mental imagery, tell your Astral
Eyes where you wish them to go and what you want them
to discover. Mentally send the Astral Eyes out on their
own. Then, bring yourself out of your altered state of consciousness to go about your usual waking routine.

At a later time, return to your altered state and sum-
mon the Astral Eyes back to you. I recommend you don't
wait more than twenty-four hours between sending it out
and bringing it back. You don't want to allow too much
time to pass since any astral creation, if not fed a fresh
supply of energy, will begin to lose momentum. After
more than a day your Astral Eyes will begin to fade, and
their power to gather information and to effectively
transfer it back to you will be impaired.

After you are back in your altered state, will your Astral
Eyes to return to the place where you first formed them.
After they appear, allow them time to finish filtering into

your mind any final impressions they have picked up on their journeys, then dismantle them in the same way you would have had you actually transferred your consciousness into them. Also dismantle the rope connecting the Astral Eyes to you. You may wish to visualize it being pulled back into your third eye, or you can allow it to fade and sink into the earth beneath you.

Remain in your altered state, focusing your attention on the impressions you have received. You'll be surprised how accurate they are. For some unknown reason, impressions and visions gained by this method seem to better correspond to events that take place in physical world time and are easier to verify than with other types of astral projection. Still, it is wise not to be overly critical of your effort should you find there is no immediate correspondence between astral and physical world events.

Tips and Suggestions for the General Transfer of Consciousness Method

Even if you eventually discover other methods of astral projection that work better for you, I heartily recommend that, as a beginner, you spend some time practicing with the general transfer of consciousness into a Body of Light. This technique will not only impress on you the full concept of shifting consciousness, but it is a good experience for timid astral travelers who want no more at first than to just float around the room in which they are reposing and reassure themselves they are really going to be all right. Through this experimentation you will gain important skills and astral self-confidence.

Each method of astral projection has uses to which it is best suited. I've found that the transfer of consciousness into a Body of Light works best for those who want to travel in the present to places already known to them or places that are not more than several hundred miles distant. It also works well for those trying to divine information about a distant loved one who might otherwise be unable to communicate. For some reason, the Body of Light method seems to make the astral body visible to those who are psychically sensitive, and such a partner may be able to confirm actually seeing or sensing you nearby.

There are several ways to help yourself succeed at this method. In general, you will find that most incenses that are known to assist in general altered state work will be of use here as well. Among these are wormwood[1], sandalwood, jasmine, or poplar bark. A mild tea of mugwort[2], catnip[3], or valerian can also be useful, but be aware that none of these taste very good. The catnip and valerian can also be strongly sedating, and the latter smells horrible if not infused with a little peppermint. Whatever you use, make sure you vary it slightly so you don't grow dependent on it. If you're unsure about how these dependencies can develop, you should read chapter 1 again.

If your goal is solely to send out your Astral Eyes, try burning a purple, blue, or silver candle between the time you send out your Astral Eyes and the time you call it back. Be sure to use caution with candles—never leave them unattended. These colors are associated with psychic perception. Having the energy of the flame combined with the color energies, which will be further

1. Wormwood is a mild cannabis that is toxic if consumed excessively.
2. Mugwort should not be used during pregnancy.
3. Catnip should not be used during pregnancy.

impressed on your mind as you see the candle burning, will strengthen the link between your third eye and the Astral Eyes. Another tip is to charge or "program" pieces of silver to help your psyche absorb the information being sent back from the Astral Eyes. To program them, hold them in your hands, infusing them with your personal energy while you focus on aligning them with your goal. Do this for several nights before trying to use them as aids in astral projection. The pieces of silver can then be worn or placed on the third eye area at any time during the Astral Eyes projection.

Summary Statements

It should be clear to you after reading this chapter that these occult techniques have uses far beyond general astral projection. They are a firm foundation on which you can build your psychic skills, and they can teach you important concepts about the nature of astral sight and movement that will continue to assist you as you gain experience.

The five astral projection methods outlined in the following chapters all build on this one in some way. If you are not yet comfortable with the practices and ideas in this chapter, continue to work with them. Your time will not be wasted.

CHAPTER 6

Astral Projection Method 2: Projecting through the Chakras

The seven chakras are energy centers that run up and down the spinal center of the physical body (as discussed in chapter 2). They are popular points of exit for those seeking to astral project. For years, battles have raged among practitioners over the best or safest chakra to use, but the truth is that any of them can work for you depending on your personal affinities and physical condition. If you need a reminder of where each chakra is located within the body, please refer to the figure on page 31.

Some astral travelers believe that exiting out of any of the lower chakras (solar plexus, navel, or root) will propel you instantly into the lower astral realms, but that projecting from the crown chakra will send you into the presence of the Godhead, or realm of the deities. But there is a popular book on the art that strongly advises the use of the solar plexus chakra due to its connection with personal willpower and its central location on the body. Another book, teaching feminist occult ideology, suggests that the navel chakra is best, especially for women. A friend of mine insists that she can only get her astral self out from the back of her neck, an area connected with the throat chakra. At different times I have used all the chakras for astral projection and, though some seem to make it easier for me than others, due to personal affinities, all of them have worked and not one has preconditioned me to end up in a place I did not want to be.

What *will* precondition you to trouble is any preconceived ideas that you carry into the experience with you. If you are absolutely convinced that exiting through the navel chakra will propel you immediately into the lower astral worlds, then that is precisely what will happen. This has to do, again, with the fluid nature of the astral plane. In this world of emotion, where thought is instantly translated into action, this should not come as a surprise.

The chakra you select to begin your experimentation should be based on your personal feelings about its energy, with consideration of any physical ailments related to that chakra. If you have a health problem connected with a certain chakra, that chakra's energy is not going to be as strong as another might be; therefore, it might be harder to utilize its psychic energy as an exit point for your astral consciousness.

The following chart is a list of energies and common illnesses associated with each chakra; the presence of any of these illnesses may indicate that the related chakra could have some blockages or a temporarily depleted energy flow. Please be aware that this is *not* a chart for diagnosing and treating your physical ailments. Its purpose is to help you determine which chakra is your strongest. The strongest chakra (of course, you may have several strong chakras) is the best candidate for your initial astral projection experiments. If you recognize your own symptoms in the "ailments" category, then the associated chakra may be weakened.

Gauging Chakra Strength

Chakra	Energies	Ailments
root	sexual, atavistic, grounding	spastic colon, chronic stomach upset, weight fluctuations, arthritis
navel	willpower, desire	depression, infertility, chronic indigestion
solar plexus	acquisitiveness, generosity	blood disorders, diabetes, paranoia
heart center	love	emotional imbalances, allergies, heart disorders, blood pressure problems

continued

Chakra	Energies	Ailments
throat	communication	throat disorders, ear and hearing problems, lung ailments, chronic colds, and hoarseness
third eye	psychicism	eye disorders, sleep disorders, dental problems, headaches, snoring, and the "new" diseases of Chronic Fatigue Syndrome and Fibromyalgia
crown	connection to the higher self	mental disorders, chemical imbalances, many cancers, neurological disorders, memory loss

Once you have selected a chakra to use in your astral projection experiment, go back to the chakra balancing and cleansing meditation on page 30. Memorize the steps so that you can bring those skills to bear in the chakra method of astral projection.

The Chakra Method of Astral Projection

To begin, go to the private, quiet place where you will be practicing your astral projection. Make whatever initial preparations you wish: light incense, undress, don a talisman, turn on some gentle music, turn up the heat to keep yourself warm, etc. Get into the body posture you have chosen to work in, then take a few moments to make sure you are comfortable enough to maintain this position for up to an hour. If not, make any desired changes now. If you decide to shift your posture later, you may unintentionally slip out of your altered state, or break your flow of visualization in a disruptive way. Once you are skilled at projecting, you will have some leeway with shifting your physical self around while still maintaining the majority of your focus on the astral experience—but for beginners this is usually disruptive.

Close your eyes and take a few deep, slow breaths. As you begin to release physical tension, also release any negative thoughts, feelings, or intentions from your mind. With each breath, feel yourself relaxing and being freed from negative energies of any kind. You may wish to visualize this in the manner of a progressive relaxation, as discussed on page 12.

Continue to breathe slowly, making sure that every part of your physical self is fully relaxed. As a beginner you may need to spend ten or twenty minutes focusing on each individual part of the body and specifically willing it to unwind. Until you are used to the sensation of total relaxation, you may not realize that certain small muscle groups are still tense unless you focus exclusively on them and work on relaxing them. If you need to review the steps in this progressive relaxation, please refer to chapter 1. There is no need to rush this process. Take as long as you need.

When you feel fully relaxed and peaceful, begin to use whatever method you have chosen or the one that works best for you to attain an altered state of consciousness. At this point, don't worry about how deep into an altered state you are able to go. Astral projection doesn't require an ultra-deep state. For now just go to the level where it feels most natural for you to be. With time and practice your altered state will come easier and will allow you to go deeper. Again, don't rush. Take all the time you need to feel that you are in the right place before continuing on.

When you feel fully relaxed, turn your attention to balancing your chakras, as described in the meditation on page 30. Pay special attention to energizing, cleansing, and balancing the one you wish to work with during this exercise.

After you have completed the chakra balancing exercise, spend some time feeling the unimpeded flow of etheric energy running through your body. Some people like to visualize this as a line of colored, highly active light racing back and forth between the chakras; others see it as a flow of high-vibration energy connecting them to the universal energies high above them. By taking time to do this, you further open the chakra centers and establish them at all levels of your being as channels to the worlds beyond your physical body.

At this point, you need to turn your consciousness as deep inside yourself as you can. Feel it sinking back into your head, flowing away from those places you usually perceive as the centers of your consciousness. Spending time visualizing your mind as an unlimited universe through which your consciousness is falling helps in the process. Allow this conscious energy to collect at the area of the chakra that you intend to use as an exit from your physical self. As you do this, try to shift your point of view from your head—the mind and eye area—to the chosen chakra's point on your body. During this process you may start to feel detached from the rest of your being, a physical numbness telling you that you have truly sent the essence of yourself to only one spot on your body. The rest of your body will be a void, a vacuum emptied of its conscious awareness.

Keeping your conscious point of view at the chakra opening, mentally energize and further open the chosen chakra by visualizing this taking place as you will it to. I like to visualize this like a round door that opens from the center outward, inviting me to slip through.

Next, you should mentally will your consciousness to slip through the chakra opening. Like the general transfer of consciousness method discussed in the previous chapter, it is recommended that after you push through the chakra, you should immediately will yourself to be someplace significant. Don't wait to see if you're "really there," on the other side of the chakra doorway, to make this shift in consciousness to somewhere else. Waiting only creates body-consciousness, which is at odds with your goal. Furthermore, mentally following the progress of the astral self out of the body hearkens back to that nearly impossible lift-out method discussed in the previous chapter. So, as soon as you slip through and start to feel the separation of body and mind, immediately will yourself elsewhere.

One possible "elsewhere" is the Body of Light. You can use this chakra technique in conjunction with the general transfer of consciousness method from chapter 4, using the Body of Light as your immediate destination. Or send yourself anywhere else in time or space that you wish to visit. It doesn't matter where you choose to go, just go somewhere to avoid hanging around in that netherland between the body and the astral plane. As a beginner you may find that familiar places are the easiest to access, but there is no harm in being adventurous, and you just may succeed. Many do.

I have found that this method of astral projection allows me excellent access to any physical place in the current time frame . . . give or take a few hours for that annoying time distortion phenomenon. I also found this was not the best method for traveling easily into the more fanciful reaches of the astral plane, such as the faery realm. I haven't compared notes on this particular method with very many other experienced projectors, so this may just be my own experience. Whatever you experience, please record it for future reference so that you know what does and does not work best for you.

You may astral travel for as long as you like. When you are ready to end your projection, shift your consciousness back to the chakra from which you exited. The simple act of focused will is all you need to make this happen. You will find yourself back inside your body, just inside the chakra opening. Visualize the opening to the chakra shutting part way, then allow a few moments to feel your consciousness ease away from the chakra area in a reversal of the way you took it there in the first place. Allow it to filter back through the vacuum of your body.

As the concentration of energy around the chakra region fades, begin to regain an awareness of your physical self. Feel your consciousness dispersing throughout your body, settling primarily in the mind and eye area where most of us conceptualize our awareness living under normal circumstances.

When you feel grounded in your physical self again, focus on each chakra area, starting from the crown and working your way down to the root. With visualization, partially close down each chakra's energy flow. As you do this, allow yourself to have a sense of slowing in the exchange of energy coming both in and out of you. Be careful that you don't close them down too much. You don't want any of them blocked so much that they impede the flow of beneficial energy, but you don't want to go around with any fully opened to allow everything in that comes your way. Doing this will result in mental or physical imbalances at worst, or might just make you feel light-headed or cranky.

After you partially shut down the chakras, permit yourself to acknowledge your head and neck, your chest and stomach, and work your way down to your feet and toes. Once you are aware of all these parts, begin to flex your hands and feet and slowly open your eyes. The last step in this returning process is to seal the portal you have created between the worlds by doing something to celebrate your corporeal self. Make noise, eat, have safe sex, or do anything else that affirms your physical existence. You may wish to ground yourself by touching the ground and visualizing excess energy fading away from you.

When you are fully back and functioning in the physical, be sure to record your experiences, successes, failures, and any other impressions in your astral journal for later reference.

Tips and Suggestions for the Chakra Projection Method

Using the chakras as an exit point seems to help people who want to feel that the power to project is within them, but need something specific to focus on in order to make the shift in consciousness. This astral projection method works well for goals relating to specific chakras or for working with the chakras in the astral. An example of this is when you leave your body to go out and practice an art known as remote healing (chapter 12 covers this fully), which involves cleansing and balancing someone else's chakra points.

The tools you should choose to assist you with the chakra method depend on which chakra you wish to exit from. Burning candles that match the chakra colors (refer to the chart on page 32) can help—as long as you have a safe way to burn them while your attention is focused elsewhere. A large fireproof basin is a good place. Incenses, metals, gems, and anointing oils can be tailored to each chakra. The latter two should be used directly on the physical chakra points whenever practical. Also, certain scents are known to stimulate and open specific energy centers. Some suggestions are provided here, but any book on occult herbalism and perfumery, aromatherapy, or on the occult properties of stones can give you many more ideas. Check the Bibliography for some recommended titles.

Chakra Associations for Tools

Chakra	Scents	Metals and Gems
root	patchouli, cypress, honeysuckle, primrose	lodestones, pewter, obsidian, onyx
navel	vanilla, yarrow, camphor, anise, hibiscus	tin, aluminum, coral, beryl, pearls, bloodstone, geodes
solar plexus	bay, cinnamon, nutmeg, lemon, frankincense	iron, amber, topaz, pyrite, bronze, Tiger's Eye
heart center	lily of the valley, hazel, bistort, lavender, almond, lemongrass, pine	copper, emerald, jasper (all colors), malachite, rose quartz
throat	benzoin, clove ginger, vervain	aquamarine, peridot, lapiz, jade
third eye	mistletoe, lilac, saffron, tuberose sandalwood	silver, moonstone, quartz, mother of pearl, sapphire
crown	sage, tobacco, hyssop, yucca, broom, lotus	opal, diamond, gold, platinum, amethyst

CHAPTER 7

Astral Projection
Method 3: Meditating
toward Astral Separation

I believe that the meditation method is one of the easiest ways to achieve astral projection. It requires more time but considerably less effort than other methods. Meditation has been defined both as "focused thought" and as "the absence of thought." During the meditative process, the body is relaxed as if in sleep, but the mind is fully alert—even though the cycles per second on which it functions are measurably slower compared to those of normal, waking consciousness. This condition allows your mind to become very receptive and open to suggestions, ideas, impressions, other intelligences, and other realms of existence.

Using Meditation to Achieve Dual Consciousness

The art of basic meditation was reviewed in chapter 1 and should be reviewed again before trying to use it as a springboard into the astral plane—especially if this process is still new to you. Achieving these meditative or altered states of consciousness is a prerequisite for most occult endeavors. It should be practiced regularly if you wish to succeed in astral projection.

A fortunate side effect of meditation is that the body grows increasingly detached from its mental processes the longer the meditative state is retained, creating the potential for achieving dual consciousness. When the body is kept in an unrelieved relaxed position for a long period of time, the mind grows bored with the body's inactivity and automatically seeks separation from it. The result: a perfectly natural astral projection.

I was using this method the first time I was successful at astral projection. At the time I was participating in a psychic development seminar in a hotel conference room in northern Arizona with about three hundred other people. The purpose of the particular session I was in was to indulge in a past-life regression extravaganza to no less than five different situations or time periods. Needless to say, it was a lengthy amount of time to spend in an altered state.

Somewhere around the third past life we were explor-ing, I grew tired of the experiment. I was not getting the clear imagery that I associate with good regression sessions, and my historian's brain was in a hopeless state of overdrive, seeking out glaring anachronisms. At the same time, I was unwilling to bring myself out of the deep-level altered state in which I found myself.

A duality of mind and body consciousness had manifested and, though I was very detached from my physical self, I was also aware enough of my body to know that my fingers and hands were completely numb from being so long in a relaxed and immobile state. As tempting as it was, I resisted the urge to twitch even one muscle, then willed myself to further forget the rest of my rapidly numbing body and continue wandering in the altered state.

It needs to be made clear at this point that the body numbness was not the result of poor circulation. I was perfectly comfortable. I was not sitting with any crossed arms or legs, nor was I in any position in which stresses could occur to press on nerves or arteries. The numbness was the direct result of the beginning of separation of body and astral consciousness.

I could feel the altered state deepen as I let go of the physical and allowed myself to drift in an inner world without thought or form. I felt myself swaying, as if some ethereal double who had been sitting inside of me was working its way out. At this point my sense of body and spirit blurred and I almost felt as if my physical self might also be rocking back and forth with the astral self.

Then, suddenly, I realized that I could see the entire conference room—from the perspective of the ceiling. I was having what occultists call a "classic" astral projection experience in which one suddenly finds oneself looking down on the physical body.

When I realized what was happening, I became so excited that I found my consciousness instantly back in my body. I kept as calm as I could, took a few deep breaths, and willed my consciousness back up to the ceiling. Soon I was rewarded with the panoramic sight of the room beneath me again. Most of the lights were off. There was a soft glow of light coming from the back of the room—the kind you might see in a movie theater—and all the people looked as if they'd just passed out as they lay strewn about the room. Some were sitting, some reclining, and all were completely still as they enjoyed their regression visions.

That was all very interesting to me, but I wanted more. I wanted to look around and see as much of the conference hall as I could so that when I opened my physical eyes again I could verify what I was seeing. As soon as I started to turn my astral self in another direction I found myself back in my body again.

I was ready to scream. I was finally able to get out of my self and stay out, but I seemed unable to do anything with this new talent I'd discovered.

I again willed myself to the ceiling, this time resolving to stay very still, and try to see and memorize all that I could. I found that if I just stayed where I was and used that dubious blessing of 360-degree sight, also called omniscient sight, which we are gifted with in the astral, that I could see everything I wanted to see. As I continued to visually peruse the room, I noticed I was able to actually look through the wall separating the conference room from the corridor outside.

When I opened my eyes, well ahead of the end of session, I looked around and was able to verify everything that I'd seen from the ceiling without any apparent time distortion effects. This absence of a time problem was probably attributable to the speaker who was leading the past-life regression, whose voice I was able to hear all the time and who probably provided a link to a specific time reference in both worlds.

Be aware that this method of astral projection takes longer to work than others, not in terms of the number of weeks or months you have to practice to be successful, but in terms of the amount of time you will have to spend each session. It takes at least thirty minutes for the body of a beginner to numb to the point where the mind will look elsewhere for entertainment. Practice will decrease this amount of time considerably, but for now be willing to make the commitment to at least an hour to ninety minutes a day. On the plus side, it is easy and relaxing and requires less effort than most methods.

The Meditation Astral Projection Process

Go to the private, quiet place you have chosen in which to practice your astral projection. Make whatever preparations you wish: light incense, undress, don a talisman, turn on some gentle music, turn up the heat to keep yourself warm, etc. Get into the body position you have chosen to work in, be it sitting or lying down. Take a few moments to make sure you are comfortable enough to maintain this position for an hour or more. If not, make your changes now. With this method, any stresses will make themselves sorely felt later on and may impede your progress.

Close your eyes and take a few deep, slow breaths. As you begin to release physical tension, also release any negative thoughts, feelings, or intentions from your mind. With each breath, feel yourself relaxing and being freed from negative energies of any kind. You may wish to visualize this in a way that has meaning for you through progressive relaxation.

Continue to breathe slowly, making sure that every part of your physical self is fully relaxed. As a beginner, you may need to spend ten or twenty minutes focusing on each individual part of the body and specifically willing it to unwind. This type of progressive relaxation is more essential to success in this method of astral projection than the others, since total relaxation of the body is a prerequisite for projecting. There is no need to rush the relaxation process. Take as long as you need to do it right.

When you are feeling fully relaxed and peaceful, begin to use whatever method you have chosen to attain an altered state of consciousness. At this point, don't worry about how deep into this state you are able to go. Just go where it feels most natural for you to go at this time.

As you continue to sit or lie quietly without moving your body, you will find that your altered state will naturally deepen, as long as you can keep your mind from wandering to mundane matters. This is probably the hardest thing to overcome. If you can't control your random thoughts, you will end up falling asleep and wasting your efforts. I find the best way to deal with this is to have some word or phrase to say over and over to yourself, coupled with a simple mental image such as a basic geometric shape (see *Focusing Your Will* on page 14). The combination of mental sight and sound will be lulling to your mind and give it something concrete, if meaningless, to focus on.

After some time passes, you will sense your body starting to go numb, and your first reaction will be to twitch a muscle or flex something. Don't! Simply take note of the lack of feeling and let it go, turning your consciousness inward and away from any physical sensations, or rather the lack of them. Allow your mind to drift. This is not an aimless drifting, but one in which you are seeking the deepest altered state you are capable of achieving at this moment.

Attempt to seek a place within you so deeply hidden that it's devoid of sight, sound, or sensation. At this point you may start to feel that telltale swaying sensation or see a host of colored lights dancing in front of your inner eyes. Don't try to force your consciousness out of your body—allow it to separate when it is ready. Try to be as detached as possible, controlling the events with a sense of will-less will.

Once you realize that you are able to see the room around you, or perhaps that of some other place nearby, you are astral projecting. Memorize all that you can see so that you are able to verify it later. If, like me during my first time, you find that moving about brings your consciousness back into yourself, simply will it gently out again to the same place it was when you returned. Don't try to send it elsewhere just yet, but let it go back up to that place it already knows. It may take many sessions for you to gain control over the astral self so that you can take it to other places, but it will come.

When you are ready to end your astral projecting session, simply shift your point of view back to your physical self. You should now reverse any process that you used to enter your altered state. If you counted breaths, begin counting them again, only this time with the idea of coming up to normal consciousness rather than going down into an altered one. If you counted numbers down, count them up. If you traveled through a cave or over a rainbow, reverse the process now. This keeps your conscious, rational mind happy as your astral mind makes the transfer back to normalcy.

Begin now to regain an awareness of your physical body. Allow yourself to acknowledge your head and neck, your chest and stomach, etc. Work your way down to your feet. Once you have reversed the process and are aware of all your body parts again, begin to flex your hands and feet and slowly open your eyes. Don't try to stand too quickly after this. You have been in a deep state of meditation, possibly for as long as ninety minutes, and you need some time to adapt to the beta-level world again. Standing suddenly will make you dizzy and could produce a host of other non-harmful but less than pleasant sensations.

The last step in this returning process is to seal the portal you have created between the worlds by doing something to celebrate your corporeal self. Make noise, eat, have safe sex, or do anything else that affirms your physical existence. You may wish to touch the ground or visualize excess energy fading away from yourself. The grounding process is important to your psychic well-being. Don't skimp on it.

Don't forget to record your experiences, successes, failures, and other impressions in your astral journal for later reference.

Tips and Suggestions for the Meditation Astral Projection Process

Review chapter 1 for tips and suggestions relating to general meditation. These will be helpful to you when using this method of astral projection. It may also help to incorporate the use of an incense that is geared toward assisting meditation or general astral projection. These suggestions have been discussed in previous chapters.

The meditation method seems to work very well if your astral projection goals concern past-life viewing, creative problem-solving (this will be covered in chapter 13), or if you simply wish to achieve a gentle separation of your astral and physical bodies and be surprised by the outcome.

To help you gauge your progress with this method, check the time just before you begin, and again just after you finish. This will give you some idea of the amount of time it takes for this method to work for you. As your skill level increases, the time elapsed will decrease significantly until the process takes no more time than any other astral projection technique.

Summary Statements

Keep in mind that in the beginning, sessions using this method will take significantly longer than they would using other methods. You'll have to be willing to double the time per day you would otherwise devote to your astral projection practice. If you have the time, this method is worth the investment. Once mastered, it can seem almost effortless in comparison to other methods.

CHAPTER 8

Astral Projection
Method 4:
Guided Meditation

Of all the methods by which one can achieve astral projection, guided meditation is undoubtedly my favorite. It combines the fluidity of the dream state with the manageability of controlled consciousness. It is as accessible as your imagination and just as limitless. Guided meditation is similar to general meditation, but it distinguishes itself in the context of astral projection by providing you with specific parameters for your exploration. This can be a big help in both entering and exiting the astral world, and can jump-start astral visions when they are slow in coming.

By the term "guided" I mean having on hand a pre-pared script, a detailed outline to follow, which uses strong symbolic language or imagery, commonly referred to as *archetypes,*[1] to lead our relaxed minds into what-ever astral world we have created for it. While in a light altered state, we follow this pre-selected imagery into the astral plane and into those areas we have chosen to explore via our meditation. Once the mind gets used to exploring the astral plane within the guidelines of the prepared meditation, you will find that it is soon able to strike out on its own. You will only need a guided script for entering and exiting the astral plane. The rest of your astral journey will be up to you.

A guided pathway to help you return to your body is a good thing to have on hand if fear of getting lost is an issue for you. Guided meditation provides a secure framework for exploration, which makes nervous travel-ers more comfortable. It's like having a well-marked map of your trip before you leave home. Side trips can be taken at your discretion, but you still always know your way back to the main road. As you become more profi-cient at guided meditation—and at getting into and out of a scene quickly and competently—you will grow bored with its confines and find yourself venturing off the path more and more, exploring the astral world on your own. The result: a fully controlled, conscious astral projection!

At first, guided meditations feel like no more than lying around with your eyes closed while someone reads a pleasant little story to you. Indeed, this may be what it

---

1. Psychologist C. G. Jung (1875–1961) introduced the term *archetypes* as a reference to prototypical situations or scenarios.

is the first time or two; but over time you will notice that you suddenly *are* where the meditation is taking place. You are experiencing the scene, rather than merely witnessing it from above. You are seeing unexpected characters in the surroundings with whom you can interact.

Your imagination is the key to making this type of projection work. If you are someone who is normally able to become deeply absorbed in your daydreams, this method of projection will not be a problem. Detractors of the guided meditation method claim that the imagination factor invalidates the experience, making it something other than a genuine astral projection. The problem with their criticism is that they automatically assume that the inner, or "imaginary," world is somehow less real than any other. Occultists have long accepted that the mind is a universe unto itself, and that what takes place there is very real. Think about the implications in terms of human civilization; all things that humankind has created had to first be constructed within the mind, made manifest as a single astral thoughtform.[2]

Another criticism of this technique is that, once mastered, it allows you to shift the bulk of your consciousness from one state to the other and back again rapidly. This should not be seen as a negative, but as a sign that you are in full control of the direction of your consciousness. In other words, this is a desirable skill that testifies to your occult dexterity, not a drawback. It is also a skill that can be employed in a variety of situations where more traditional forms of astral projection are not possible. For example, when I was a college freshman stuck in a boring job where thinking was not a requirement, I used a variation of this type of astral projection as an

2. See Glossary.

escape from the drudgery. At times I was 70 percent in the astral world and 30 percent in the physical, other times the proportions were switched, but being able to switch back and forth between the worlds permitted me to keep working while maintaining my sanity.

None of these criticisms tell us that the guided meditation method does not result in a true astral projection experience. Experienced occultists are well aware of the dual nature of the human consciousness and of its tendency to shift back and forth in perspective during virtually all types of projection. In *Esoteric Rune Magic* (Llewellyn, 1994), occult magician D. Jason Cooper writes that during astral projection, an awareness of both worlds is always present; we "simply ignore [the physical] in favor of the vision [we] behold." In *Time Travel: A New Perspective* (Llewellyn, 1997), J. H. Brennan theorizes that any meditative discipline may actually be allowing us to experience "two parallel *realities*" (emphasis mine). He states that:

> . . . the means by which this may be done is the human imagination, a psychological function devalued by most of us . . . When you use imagination . . . you are actually gazing into another world, a time-space continuum different from the physical reality around you, but just as objective, just as real.[3]

When your imagination is engaged in something, so are your emotions. Because astral projection is above all else an exercise of emotional consciousness, guided meditation provides a sturdy springboard into the astral world.

I know from experience that what starts out as a fantasy projection tends to take on a life of its own as we

3. J. H. Brennan. *Time Travel: A New Perspective* (St. Paul, MN: Llewellyn Worldwide, 1997) 166.

progress through the astral experience. I have also been able to use some of these projections as tools for creative visualization, encouraging things to manifest for me on the physical plane (I'll address visualization fully in chapter 13). If the plane that my mind engages in is not real, how then am I able to plant ideas and desires there that later manifest in the physical world—the only reality most other people acknowledge? Where there is no fertile soil, there can be no harvest; and where there is a harvest, there must be fertile soil.

Finding Guided Meditation Scripts

You can find some very good guided meditation scripts in a variety of occult books, especially those that are written from a Pagan or nature-religion perspective. I highly recommend Yasmine Galenorn's *Trancing the Witch's Wheel* (Llewellyn, 1997). This beautiful book is not just for those who follow the religion of Wicca, but for anyone who wishes to gain a deeper understanding of the seasons and the elements via guided meditation. The symbolic language used in these scripts is excellent, and the storylines are cohesive and engaging. For those of you who want to use a meditation that is already written out for you, this is an excellent place to start.

Another way to find guided meditation scripts is by delving into fairy tales. These are strongly symbolic, and usually involve a successful hero or heroine going into an unfamiliar world inhabited by strange beings. Some are allies and some are enemies. The hero or heroine must discover which is which while navigating the alien landscape and its unfamiliar rules, then return home with some sort of prize. You will need to pick your fairy tales with care. An excess of dark imagery is not good for beginners. Although dark images are not inherently harmful, they often contain too much volatile energy for new travelers on the astral plane to handle wisely. Save these for later, when you are prepared to use them to your best advantage. For the same reason, you should stay away from tales with unpleasant endings. Stick with the "and they lived happily ever after" endings for now.

Writing Your Own Guided Meditations

Learning to write your own guided meditations geared to your current spiritual goals is not hard if you're willing to gain some knowledge of archetypes and symbolism,[4] information easily found in books on psychology for the layman, some dream interpretation guides, and in many occult books. In general terms, we are using the term *archetype* to refer to an ideal example of a certain type of situation, time, or condition. For our purposes, a *symbol* is an object that represents that archetype.

Remember that your mind as a whole responds best to symbolic language. In fact, this is the only language that your subconscious mind can understand, and it must be fully engaged for guided meditation to work as a means to astral project. On the other hand, the symbolism in your meditation should not be so dense that it interferes with the flow of the story framework on which the imagery is hung.

I have compiled a brief list of commonly used archetypes below. These should assist you in writing your own guided meditations if you so desire. You may discover

4. The works of C. G. Jung are particularly useful. Look for *Archetypes and the Collective Unconscious* in any edition of Jung's compiled works.

and utilize any number of symbols and archetypes beyond this list; it is merely an introduction to the multitudes that you may eventually define.

Symbols and Archetypes for Use in Guided Meditation

Symbol	Archetype
bees	team effort, solidarity, industry
butterfly	rebirth, change, temporary calm
cat	moon, night mysteries, self-mastery, magic, fear
cave	womb (especially of the mother earth), the past, ancient mysteries, mother earth Goddess, rebirth, getting past fear
dog	fidelity, a warning or caution
door	portal between worlds
dwarf	gnomes, earth spirits, earth wisdom
egg	fertility, cycles of life, eternity, beginnings
evergreens	eternal life, health
fire	energy, transformation, transition
grains	prosperity, abundance, hospitality, comfort, celebration, fertility
horse	feminine energies, a mediator between the worlds, a facilitator of astral travel, nightmares

continued

Symbol	Archetype
key	immobility, solutions, sexuality
knife	discord, transfer of energy, distrust, warning
mountain	obstacles, facing personal challenges, spiritual quests, seeking wisdom
owl	wisdom, warning, death, elderhood
rain	gifts, blessings, fertility
rainbow	peace, a link between worlds, unity, safe passage
river	flow of time, cycles of life and death, transition from one world or time to another
serpent	feminine mysteries, change after stagnation, earth energy
stag	masculine energy, the changing seasons
tools	labor, a gift offered for a coming ordeal
tornado	major change, diminishing, banishing, decrease
tree	continuity, strength
wall	obstacles, immobility, the end of something
web	unity, connection, pathways opening, wisdom offered, industry

Ensuring Successful Guided Meditation

The rules for writing—or recognizing—a safe and effective guided meditation are simple: it should use as much archetypal symbolism as can be used without compromising the story-like feeling. You should always enter and exit the meditation by the same path, except in special circumstances such as a physical world emergency. Another exception to this rule is when the meditation has been purposely structured, for spiritual reasons, toward using a different exit point. In most cases, however, if you use the mental entry point of a cave, you should exit through that same cave. Other popular paths into the astral plane via guided meditation are rainbows, mountain pathways, wells, kivas (underground ceremonial places), and being escorted in and out by animal or spirit guides.

The middle part of your guided meditation can take you anywhere you'd like to go, in this world or any other, or into the presence of any astral being you wish to contact, including the departed souls of most human beings. Naturally, the free will of each being comes into play here, and sometimes a certain being may not feel like visiting, so don't push the issue. The imagery you use in the beginning should remain simple; don't try to project into worlds with extremely detailed scenes just yet. With this method you will usually find you progress rapidly, and the astral world will fill itself in for you very soon, surprising you with its complexity.

Another advantage of this astral projection method is that it can be custom-tailored to your needs and desires. Most guided meditation scripts include suggestions for progressive relaxation in the beginning, and for slowly coming back to waking consciousness afterward, so that both transitions are smooth and non-jarring to your mind. Language can also be included that provides you with an automatic return button (see page 65) to escape if you become frightened for any reason. The meditation script can offer what amounts to a post-hypnotic suggestion to lose or let go of any memory of an event or encounter that is not conducive to your current spiritual growth, or that will prove disturbing to your waking life.

The biggest drawback to the guided meditation method is that you will initially need to have the text read to you while you work through it. If you have a trusted partner with whom you feel you can totally relax and who has enough good instincts to know when to pause within the text to allow you to explore, that is ideal. If not, try reading the meditation into a recorder and playing it back for yourself. If you are one of those who finds the sound of your own voice distracting, you can either ask someone to record it for you, or try masking your voice qualities by mixing in some New Age music as a background to your words. It is wise to test your recording after a few minutes to make sure you are getting the right balance of voice and sound before wasting your time reading the entire meditation. I've made this mistake before, and ended up with a recording in which I could barely hear the words over the roar of the music.

A brief guided meditation script is included in this chapter. It has a structured beginning and ending, but the middle is left open so that it can be altered to suit your needs. I'm very fond of the image of a rainbow bridge into the astral, so that's what I use. You can choose to turn this image into a cave, a well, a kiva, or whatever you wish. The middle part as it is written here is short, directing you to a world in which a single astral place—in this case, a magical forest—may be explored. If you wish to make this portion of the meditation longer, simply instruct your reader to allow more quiet time at this point, or do so yourself when you record it. You should also feel free to write your own pathway for the middle section so that you can explore areas of the astral plane which are of most interest to you. When you are done doing this, you need only return to the main body of the meditation to find your way home again.

The Guided Meditation Projection Process

To begin, go to the private, quiet place you have chosen to practice your astral projection. Make whatever initial preparations you wish: light incense, undress, don a talisman, turn on some gentle music, turn up the heat to keep yourself warm, etc. Get into the body posture you have chosen to work in and take a few moments to make sure you are comfortable enough to maintain this position for up to an hour. If not, make your adjustments now. You don't want to disrupt your flow of visualization by doing it later.

Close your eyes and take a few deep, slow breaths. As you begin to release physical tension, also release any negative thoughts, feelings, or intentions from your mind. With each breath, feel yourself relaxing and being freed from negative energies of any kind.

Continue to breathe slowly, making sure that every part of your physical self is fully relaxed. As a beginner you may need to spend ten or twenty minutes focusing on each individual part of the body and willing it specifically to unwind. Until you are used to the sensation of total relaxation, you may not realize that certain small muscle groups are still tense unless you focus exclusively on them and work on relaxing them. There is no need to rush. Take as long as you need.

When you are relaxed and feeling peaceful, begin the guided meditation. The script follows.

Guided Meditation: Sample Script

Visualize the end of a large, vivid rainbow appearing before you. See your astral self standing at its base, feeling the positive vibrations that the rainbow gives off. As you step up onto the rainbow, you suddenly become lighter than air and fly along its surface, moving with increasing speed toward its apex, so high above you that you cannot see it. You have no temptation to look below you and see the world you are leaving behind, but only to look ahead at the dazzling light show emanating from the rainbow.

As you travel upward, the atmosphere around you grows lighter and whiter. You feel the tensions, problems, concerns, and petty negativities of your physical world, which have been encasing you like a suit of armor, break off and fall away from you. You find that you now feel

freer than you ever have before, and you are
filled with positive, spiritual energy.

As you reach the apex of the rainbow, you
shout for joy at the feeling of freedom that
engulfs you, and your flight follows the rainbow's wide curve and begins its trip downward
into the astral world.

Down, down you fly, though a world that grows
always lighter. A sacredness almost seems to
permeate the atmosphere in which you soar.
Soon you see below you a vast, verdant expanse
that looms ever wider, seemingly without end.
As you fly faster, coming ever closer, you see it is
a beautiful, unspoiled forest.

You slow near the rainbow's end until you come
to a stop, stepping off onto the soft, green-
brown soil of the forest floor. As you stand, getting your bearings, you recognize this to be an
enchanted forest, filled with magical creatures,
and you know that here, anything is possible.

The bright sunlight is muted to shades of twi-
light as it peers down through the heavy
foliage. As you look up, you notice flashes of
golden light that seem to come from small tree

spirits in the boughs over your head. Off to your left is a small rock outcropping with a tiny fissure you presume to be a cave. To your right you can hear the sounds of running water, as in a fast moving river. Animals peep through the trees to regard you curiously, and seem to be conferring among themselves as to what you might want here in their special world.

Without warning, you hear a voice behind you, and you spin to seek the source, but you can see no one there—only the tree, which in this magical place could actually be speaking.

The voice directs you to look up, where you see, sitting on the branch of a large and ancient tree, an owl with huge blinking eyes. Though its beak does not move, you are clearly aware of every word it telepathically transmits to you.

At this point you can allow your visit with the owl to be enough, or you can continue, following a prepared meditation or your own investigations. Suggestions for additions to this meditation are meeting with a wizard in a clearing, meeting with water faeries at a woodland lake, sailing down an astral river that passes through the forest, talking with animals or plants, meeting forest spirits and faeries, interacting with other nature spirits, or meeting with your guides and teachers. You can also take off for other places in the astral world and enjoy whatever time, place, setting, or company you wish.

Always do what feels most comfortable to you each time you use this method to project. When you are ready to end this session, continue with the following rainbow bridge imagery to return to your normal consciousness.

> **Visualize the end of the rainbow returning to you. As you step up onto it, you will find you can fly, and will follow the arch up to its apex again. At the top, you will start your descent. As you go back down, note that the atmosphere around you grows denser and sparkles with less color. Continue to fly faster down the rainbow until you see the world that you left looming beneath you.**

Slow your descent until you come to a stop at the rainbow's end, somewhere in the vicinity of your body. Step off and mentally transfer your consciousness back into your physical self.

After you feel fully back inside of yourself, visualize the rainbow fading back into the astral world and begin to regain an awareness of your physical body. Slowly, and one by one, acknowledge your head and neck, your chest and stomach, and work your way down to your feet. Once you are aware of all these parts, begin to flex your hands and feet and slowly open your eyes.

The last step in this returning process is to seal the portal you have created between the worlds by doing something to celebrate your corporeal self. Make noise, eat, have safe sex, or do anything else that affirms your physical existence. Visualize excess energy fading away from yourself. Because this method requires more mental and emotional stimulation than most other methods, the potential to haunt yourself with excess energy is greater, so don't skimp on the grounding process.

Don't forget to record your experiences, successes, failures, and other impressions in your magical journal or occult diary for later reference. It's also important that you record the details of the guided meditation or controlled fantasy that you used to enter the astral world. Often times these have a direct bearing on the specific place you land on the astral plane. It can also affect your initial astral experience in terms of content and direction. You may want to study these later, when you are seeking a specific type of astral projection and wish to use the exact same method of entry.

Guided Meditation and Astral Time Travel

If you are interested in using astral projection as a means of time travel, either to explore a past life or simply to peer into another era, this is by far the best method to use. The fact that time is non-linear (it is only perceived that way by our physical selves) is a concept that is now becoming known beyond the scientific and occult communities. Since all time is an omnipresent "now," it can be accessed by us at any point if we find a way to break free of the constraints of physical thinking. This truth was made clear to me several years ago when my husband and I were shopping for a new home. Even knowing we could not afford the maintenance on an antique house, I still couldn't resist going to see a beautifully pre-served circa 1901 cottage in a small town known for its well-cared for old homes. I was enchanted with the place and could not get it out of my thoughts the rest of the day. That night, as I was astral projecting, my mind wandered to the house and I instantly found myself inside it. It was as empty as I'd seen it that afternoon, but was now completely dark. I was gazing at the east end of the great room, trying to imagine what it would be like to live there, when suddenly I saw the illumination of daylight coming through the back of the house, and I found I was seeing a dual reality. The wall was still there, but I could see through it into the kitchen, which had been added in the 1930s. Two women and a girl of about ten were in there preparing a meal. I took note of as much detail as I could. The next day, I attempted to verify the images in my astral vision. It turned out that the wall I had seen through had not been there in the 1930s. The house had been updated again in the 1950s when the wall between what is now the great room and the kitchen was erected.

Most experienced astral projectors will likely agree that viewing the past is easier than viewing the future, and there are numerous ways of using the guided medi-tation method to achieve this.

Astral Time Travel: Sample Experiments

Exploring past lives through astral projection gives us the security of keeping us detached from the emotional tur-moil of a past life while still allowing us to see and understand its full implications for our current life situa-tion. If you want to astrally explore a past life, use one of the following methods to lead you to the specific era you'd like to explore. Chances are if you're drawn to a historical period enough to want to do this, then you probably lived at that time.

1. Find and study a photograph or drawing of a time past that appeals to you and, as you enter your altered state, form that image vividly in your mind. Use both your intuition and imagination to go beyond the boundaries of the picture and see what is there. Allow the mental picture to expand until it becomes a fully dimensional place, then project your consciousness into it using a transfer of consciousness technique.

2. Prepare a guided meditation containing imagery that will lead you into a scene or event in history as you imagine it to be. As you enter your altered state, follow this historical imagery. You will likely soon find yourself floating above the scene or event, watching it unfold. At first this vision will be 90 percent pure imagination, but as you improve your skills and are able to leave the prepared pathway, you will get a sense that you are running on only about 20 percent imagination.

As you watch your past unfolding, you will have to decide how long to stay on the guided pathway (until you are fully engaged in what you're seeing) and when to leave the prepared meditation to just observe the events. Prepare for this in your meditation by writing out the exact path into the time period, then reversing it to get out. Be sure to leave a large part of the middle open so that you can watch what happens. If past-life exploration is new to you, you may need to create a few scenes to jump-start the visions. Many newcomers need to do this the first several times they try astral projecting into a past life, so don't worry about it having a negative impact on the overall experience.

Tips and Suggestions for the Guided Meditation Method of Astral Projection

I began using guided meditation as a method of astral projection long before I knew what the technical name was for what I was doing. Many times I have been in bed late at night or early in the morning, asleep but not asleep, traveling in my fantasy world and having a great time. If you are someone who is given to having a rich inner life, full of vivid fantasies and daydreams, you may find that you are doing this type of projection already. If not, you will certainly find it an easy technique to learn.

Scents. Incenses can be used to help focus your astral consciousness on a specific goal when doing guided meditation. The scent of lilac has long been touted as one that helps open us to past-life experiences. Many occultists and Wiccans will place a single drop of pure lilac oil over the third eye area to help open these visions. Lilac oil also seems to work as a filter to keep out more disturbing past-life events until you are ready to handle them. The scent of anise works similarly to lilac but, in my experience, tends to attract the astral projector to viewing past lives with more violent events and unpleasant content. This does not make anise a "bad" scent to use, just one with different energies that produce a different type of vision.

Extracts. Rowan or mastic extracts have been believed to aid in time travel to the past, but both can be hard to find. You can make your own extracts out of these by boiling the herbs and then straining them to obtain the liquid. Mistletoe extract, on the other hand, can assist with projections into the future. Anoint the third eye with one of these extracts if you want to use them for astral projection.

Holey Stones. Stones with naturally occurring holes in them can be placed over the third eye to act as a portal to other times. These work exceptionally well if you intend to exit through this chakra. Holey stones have been held sacred in many cultures, seen as symbols of the birth canal of the eternal Goddess who gives birth to us again and again. The usefulness of this archetypal symbol should be obvious if you're trying to travel into another of your own lifetimes.

Summary Statements

Remember that you are always in control of where you go. If something occurs that you don't wish to witness, or you just suddenly feel the need to leave the vision, simply return to your guided pathway and follow it home. This quick route out of the astral plane is the greatest advantage of this method, so use it if need be.

CHAPTER 9

Astral Projection Method 5: Using Symbolic Gateways

The symbols used in occult and religious practices are more than pretty glyphs—they are potent symbols that have been studied and employed for thousands of years to affect a change in our consciousness. The mysteries they simultaneously offer and conceal place them at the threshold of time at a point where all worlds and times meet. Because of this, they provide us with effective gateways to the astral plane.

The method of using symbolic gateways for astral projection has been popular among many paths of occultism, particularly those involved in what is called ceremonial or high magic, a mystical system based on the Judeo-Christian and Egyptian mystery schools.

If you find yourself deeply attracted to any archetypal symbol, don't let cultural barriers prevent you from using it. Some symbols are more meaningful than others to us as individuals, and all are imbued with great occult potential.

The symbol or symbols that you select to begin your experimentation should be chosen with some caution. They need to reflect ancient, archetypal themes with which the subconscious mind can connect itself. But, for beginners, they also need to be simple enough in form and content that the mind doesn't have too many parts of an image to focus on at once.

For now, you should keep the symbol both in your mind and on paper in the form of a simple line drawing, preferably black on white, with absolutely no color variants. Full color images, such as the tarot cards or the Indian *tattwa* symbols, are frequently used by more experienced occultists, but these require an entirely different process of inner vision, and they are best saved until some experience has been gained in this area. You'll understand the reasons for this fact shortly.

Virtually any drawing or glyph that is strongly associated with a spiritual system or other aspect of occult study can become a symbolic gateway into the astral world. A chart of simple archetypal images suitable for the beginner can be found on pages 152-153.

After you have selected a symbol to begin working with, you will need to make a larger physical image of it. You will need some white poster-board, perhaps a ruler to make straight lines with, and a black marker. If you wish to hold the symbol in your hands as you sit to meditate, then your poster-board needs to be cut down to a size no more than six by six inches. If you wish to place it on a wall to gaze at as you lie down, you'll need something that is at least twenty by twenty inches. For some of the techniques described here you will also need a second piece of blank white poster-board, cut to the same size.

Carefully reproduce your chosen symbol onto the center of the poster-board, making it as geometrically accurate as you can. Use heavy, broad strokes that are clear and easy to see. Rulers, compasses, and all those other tools you used in tenth grade geometry class will come in handy for helping you make your drawing as accurate as possible. And you thought you'd never use that stuff after high school!

On the day prior to your first attempt at astral projecting through the symbol, spend at least twenty minutes getting to know it intimately. You want to know this symbol like an old friend—well enough that it triggers an immediate emotional response in you.

Gaze at it and meditate on not only its general meaning, but also on the meaning it has specifically for you. Read about its origin and history, as well as about its symbolic energies in cultures or times other than your own. Remember that this is a symbol you have chosen to use as a doorway into the astral plane, and your emotions about and conceptualization of it will directly affect the astral world that you will find yourself in with its assistance.

*Alchemical
Symbol: fire*

*Moon:
mysteries*

*Masculine
Energies*

*Alchemical
Symbol: water*

*Venus:
feminine
energy*

*Alchemical
Symbol: air*

*Pentagram:
protection, unity,
victorious spirit*

*Ankh:
life*

*Alchemical
Symbol: earth*

*Solar Wheel:
eternal earth
cycles*

*Circle:
completeness
and eternity*

*Square:
stability*

*Figure 5 (above and facing page).
Examples of Symbolic Gateways*

| *I Ching Glyph: "the wanderer"* | *Ancient Goddess Energy* | *Triple Moon: hidden change* |

| *I Ching Glyph: "pushing upward"* | *Latin Cross: ascension (Christian)* | *Solomon's Seal: unity and the creator* |

Gazing at the symbol for several minutes just prior to falling asleep is a good practice. These symbols are strong images onto which the subconscious can latch and carry into your dream world, allowing you to forge an even stronger link with them.

The subsequent dreams that you may have about your symbol could offer you special insight into its meaning—insight that you might miss if you don't choose to engage your sleep-consciousness. In some cases, people have reported that these dreams have provided a spontaneous astral projection through their chosen symbolic gateway.

All of this is part of conditioning your mind to do what you want it to do. When you take the time to properly prepare it, your mind may very well surprise you with its willingness to play along.

The Symbolic Gateway as a Portal to the Dead

Occasionally someone who has recently lost a loved one will come to me and ask about using astral projection as a means of visiting with the deceased. It is certainly possible to do this through astral projection, but success depends on several factors that are outside the control of the one doing the projecting, the most important being the willingness of the passed-over spirit to allow the contact. If someone truly wants to pursue this, I almost always recommend the symbolic gateway method as the best course of action.

Certain archetypes are strongly impressed on our psyches as being portals between worlds, particularly between the world of the living and that of the dead. These include doors, wells, caves, fissures, openings in dense cloud formations, visible rays of sunlight, and the empty spaces behind portraits that hang on walls.

Another means to contact the spirit of someone who has died is to ask your spirit guide to assist you in making the connection. Your guide can easily find out if the spirit is willing at this time to see you and, if so, will be able to lead you to the best place in the astral world for the meeting.

This will often be a spot where there is a symbolic gateway that either you or the spirit will have to step through to get to one another. Other times—and I've discovered this from my own experience—the guide will ask that you each remain on your own side of the gateway. You will still be able to make physical contact through touching, hugging, etc., but your guide will often request that your astral feet remain firmly planted on your own side of the portal.

The Symbolic Gateway Astral Projection Process

The mental imagery we use for entering the symbol itself is an old one that has fascinated our collective imagination for ages. Many of us grew up with Lewis Carroll's classic children's story *Through the Looking-Glass* (1872), in which a young woman inadvertently falls into a parallel reality on the other side of an inanimate object (the mirror). To achieve astral projection via symbolic gateway, we too will pass through an inanimate object to peer at the world on the other side.

To begin this process, have your symbol card or drawing and the blank double with you. You may hold the cards in your hand if you will be sitting with them, but if you choose to lie down, you should attach the drawing and its double side by side on the wall in front of where you will be working. This should be in your bedroom or that other private, quiet place where you practice your astral projection. The room you are in should be as dimly lit as possible while still allowing you to clearly see the symbol.

Make whatever other preparations you wish at this time: ignite incense, undress, don a talisman, turn on some gentle music, turn up the heat to keep yourself warm, etc. Get into the position you have chosen to work in. If you are sitting, hold the card with the drawing on your lap with the blank right behind it. If you are lying down, these should be side by side on the wall directly in front of your bed or other reclining area.

Take a few moments to make sure you are comfortable enough to maintain your chosen body posture for up to an hour. If not, make the desired changes now. Close your eyes and take a few deep, slow breaths. As you begin to release physical tension, also release any negative thoughts, feelings, or intentions from your mind. With each breath, feel yourself relaxing and being freed from negative energies of any kind.

Continue to breathe slowly, making sure that every part of your physical self is fully relaxed. If you need to review the steps in progressive relaxation, consult chapter 1 before you begin. There is no need to rush the process. Take as long as you need.

When you feel fully relaxed, very slowly open your eyes partially. Don't allow yourself to be jolted out of your altered state of consciousness. Just keep your gaze soft and gently focused as you begin to gaze at the symbol on your lap or wall. As a beginner you may have to shut your eyes for a few moments and try again if you feel the act of opening your eyes has jolted you out of your altered state. Take your time and don't allow yourself to become frustrated.

Once you are able to partially open your eyes and still feel that you are in an altered state, begin to gaze at the symbol you've chosen. This often works best for our purposes if you attempt to gaze *through* rather than at the symbol, as if seeking something that lies inside or beyond the physical card. This art is known as *scrying*—it is the same skill employed by a clairvoyant gazing into a crystal or a bowl of murky water to seek visions.

After several minutes the image will begin to blur around the edges, seeming to become less solid. When you reach this point, carefully transfer your gaze to the blank card you have ready. The image of the symbol should appear on the card in reverse "color." In other words, the dark parts will appear light and the light parts will appear dark. This is conceptualized as the astral part of the symbol, one that is a mirror image of the symbol's appearance in the physical world. At this point you may allow your consciousness to shift into the symbol.

If you find this is too much of a change in consciousness to handle all at once, there are several visualizations you can use to assist your consciousness through the symbolic gateway. One way is by mentally enlarging the image. Allow it to appear in its mirror image form— white where it should be black and black where it should be white—*without* opening your eyes. Visualize this happening on the inside of your eyelids. When the symbol is as large as a standard doorway, visualize yourself stepping through it.

An alternate method you can employ (one that many occultists like to use) is to visualize the mirror image dissolving into a veil, which you can then part like a curtain and step through. Or, you can visualize an actual door forming on the symbol, complete with a doorknob that you can just turn to open and enter.

Once you enter the astral plane though a symbolic gateway, you will find yourself in a part of the astral world that is directly influenced by the centuries of thoughtforms and images built up around the symbol. For example, if you chose the alchemical symbol for water, you will find yourself in a realm dominated by this element.

At first, the imagery of the plane will be as starkly simple as the symbol. You may notice that everything initially looks like a black and white film negative, with all of the light spots appearing dark and the dark spots appearing light. As you move into this world, you'll first notice that all the neutral tones are becoming the way they should be: things will slowly begin to appear in color.

Now that you have successfully entered the symbol, you do not have to remain there. You are now astral projected and can travel anywhere on the astral plane you wish to go, meet anyone you wish, and learn anything you like. Only your desire and your skill level will limit you.

When you are ready to end your projection session you should come back via the same route by which you entered. Mentally will yourself to the inside of the symbol—to the place where you first found yourself as you entered the astral world. Slip through the image and transfer your consciousness back into your body by willing it to be there. Allow your mental visions to be seen from the physical self's point of view.

Still visualizing the symbol, reverse the imagery you used to open this gateway. For example, if you allowed it to enlarge, see it shrink; if you turned it into a veil, see it become solid again. This helps seal that portal you've opened between the worlds so that one does not bleed over into and disturb the other.

Now begin to regain awareness of your physical body. One by one, recall the presence of each part of your body, starting at the toes and working your way up. Begin to flex your hands and feet and slowly open your eyes.

As always, this is the point at which you should celebrate your corporeal self. Make noise, eat, have safe sex, or do anything else that affirms your physical existence. You may wish to ground yourself, visualizing excess energy fading away.

Don't forget to record your experiences, successes, failures, and any other impressions in your astral journal for later reference.

Using Symbolic Gateways with Color

After you've gained some experience with using black and white symbolic gateways, you can try using color. The most frequently used symbols for this purpose are the tattwa symbols: geometric shapes symbolizing the elements of earth, water, fire, air, and spirit. Entering into these elemental worlds provides us a springboard to the astral plane and teaches us about the qualities of nature.

The process for entering the color symbols is basically the same as for the black and white symbol, except for one thing: a change in color will occur when you transfer your gaze from the colored symbol to the blank poster-board. If you are familiar with color relationships or have studied art, you will no doubt be familiar with the fact that shifting your gaze from a colored object to a blank white space yields a "ghost image" that appears in the original color's complement.

Complementary colors are found opposite each other on the color wheel (see Figure 6)—color film negatives appear in complementary colors, for instance. The image that appears once you transfer your gaze from the tattwa symbol to the blank card will be the same symbol in its complementary color.

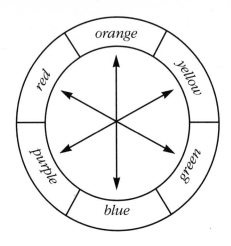

Figure 6. Complementary Colors on a Color Wheel

In the chart below, I've used the word "complement" to describe the resulting ghost image.

Tattwa Symbols and Colors

Element	Symbol	Complement
earth	yellow square	violet square
water	silver crescent	black-violet crescent
fire	red triangle	green triangle
air	blue circle	orange circle
spirit	black oval	white oval

As with the black and white symbols, as you slow your consciousness and gaze into the color symbol, you will begin to notice that it becomes hazy around the edges. You will also start to see this opposite color bordering the symbol. At this point, carefully transfer your

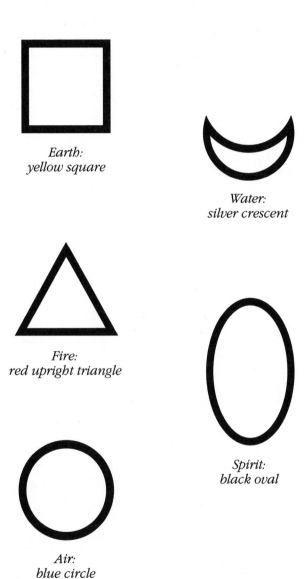

Figure 7. Tattwa Symbols

gaze to the blank card and allow the image to re-form before your eyes in its color opposite. Sometimes you will find it hard to hold the image in the center of the blank card without straining. If this happens, close your eyes for a moment and start over again.

Color symbols such as the tattwas are naturally more complex. They represent gateways to very complex parts of the astral world, so it is wise for you to jump-start your projection into them with your imagination so you end up exactly where you want to be behind that symbolic doorway.

Before you begin, have in mind some idea what might lie beyond the particular gateway you have chosen. In my first experience inside the elemental worlds entering via a symbolic gateway, I was rendered immobile by the astral world of the element in its purest form. Some other imagery or idea of what would lie ahead was needed to bring the astral world into a manageable form.

To do this, you will have to employ both this astral projection method and the guided meditation method of the previous chapter to make these work well for you. This is why it is usually not an operation for beginners. After you have success with the black and white gateways, give these a try; but allow the black and white symbols to be your training ground.

If you want to ease into the practice of using color symbols, try adding a single tint to the black and white symbol you have previously worked with. Don't agonize over this. Simply select the color that you feel best represents the symbol, and learn from that choice. No choice is going to harm you. For example, you might make the moon symbol silver, symbolic of psychic ability and feminine power. You might make the Venus glyph a vibrant, fertile green; make the Ankh symbol of life a rich, blood red; or make the Latin Cross a vivid gold.

As you make your selections, keep in mind that every element you add to your symbolic gateway is going to make it harder to hold in your mind and it will create a correspondingly complex astral world on its other side. Until you've worked up to it, stick with a single color rather than being tempted to try more.

Tarot Cards as Symbol Astral Gateways

Another symbolic gateway that is very popular with those who are experienced at using them are the tarot cards. These divination decks of ancient origin are loaded with deeply symbolic art. The complete deck is a representation of all inner and outer worlds. If you start with the Fool card and work your way through the deck, you will have taken a spiritual journey from novice to adept.

I'm not recommending that you use the tarot cards as symbolic gateways anytime soon. To do this requires superior visualization skills. You must be able to hold all the images of the card in your mind at once in both their physical and astral world color schemes. The beings you will meet on the other side will be mythic ones. They will challenge you, test you, tease you, and you will be judged fit to stay among them by your skills at turning these enemies into allies in order to capture the prize of spiritual advancement. For now, just be aware that this type of astral projection is possible in your future, and that it is very rewarding.

Another Way to Use Color

If manipulation of symbols seems too much for you now and you'd rather stick to neutral images (but you still like the idea of using color energy), try burning candles in a color that shares an affinity with the symbol you have chosen. Naturally, you should only burn candles if it can be done safely. You can focus on the energy of the *color* as opposed to the *symbol* as you enter your altered state. This is probably the safest color method, and is every bit as effective as focusing on the meaning of a symbol.

In almost any book on occult practice you can find a list of color associations for various symbols and for the elements, but most of them advise you to experiment to discover exactly what works best for you. In terms of the four elements, use these colors as guidelines for beginning your astral projection experiments.

Color Associations for Elements

Element	Colors
earth	brown, green, yellow
water	violet, silver, blue
fire	red, orange, gold
air	blue, white, gray

Tips and Suggestions for Using the Symbolic Gateways Astral Projection Method

The first few times you use this method you are going to feel as if you are making up the astral projection and are not really on the astral plane. To some extent this may be true but, like the guided meditation process discussed in the previous chapter, this is a method that can rapidly progress into a true astral projection. With practice you will soon realize that you are actually projected into the symbol and capable of taking charge of your astral self and traveling anywhere else on the astral plane you choose.

Never forget that the symbol you use as an entry point into the astral world has a direct bearing on that part of the astral world in which you initially find yourself. You will have the freedom to move from this place into other parts of the astral plane, but in most cases you will have to return to this same spot to return home. Think through your choices carefully. Be careful to choose an image that will not result in an astral place so inhospitable to you that you'll have trouble making yourself exit though that point.

At least part of that problem can be controlled by adding aspects of the guided meditation process to the symbolic one. In many cases it is almost essential that you do this, since many of the worlds these glyphs lead to are so basic in nature that they offer almost no room for exploration.

Earlier in this chapter, I mentioned my first experience entering the astral world via a symbol—the one for the element of earth. As I entered the astral plane, I found myself trapped in what was likely a small subterranean fissure deep within the earth. I could see nothing, since there is no natural light underground. No matter how long I waited, my eyes could never adjust—there was simply no illumination off of which they could bounce an image.

After a friend told me of a similar experience on entering the astral plane through an air symbol, I began experimenting with using guided imagery to create an initial world that represented the earth element, but left the experience open enough to allow for learning and further travel in the astral.

The incenses, oils, or other enhancing substances you use with the symbolic gateway process work best if tailored to the energies of the specific symbol you've chosen. For instance, in the case of symbols related to the four elements (earth, water, fire, and air), you would want to choose a scent known to be "ruled" by, or that shares an affinity with, that specific element.

Scent Associations for Elements

Element	Scents
earth	patchouli, honeysuckle, primrose, magnolia, sweet pea
water	vanilla, apple, jasmine, sandalwood, lily of the valley, lotus
fire	cinnamon, bay, clove, ginger, nutmeg, orange, rosemary, frankincense
air	sage, mint, lavender, anise, maple, evergreen, citron

For the non-elemental symbols, you'll have to do some research on your own. Books on occult herbalism and perfumery are excellent sources for beginning this research, and I recommend that any magician or occultist own at least one of these references (see Bibliography for specific titles).

Other resources can be found in books that explore the spirituality and mysticism of a particular spiritual system. For example, to research the scents and colors associated with the Ankh or the Horns of Isis, you would look into a book on Egyptian spiritual practices. A very brief list of suggestions for scents and colors corresponding to some of the more popular symbols follows. This should get you started.

Scent and Color Associations for Select Symbols

Symbol	Scents	Colors
Horns of Isis	amaranth, cinnamon, patchouli, vervain	gold, yellow, blue
Latin Cross	agrimony, hyssop, myrrh, olive	silver, gold, green
Star of David	acacia, allspice, bay, thyme	violet
pentagram	bay, sage, rosemary, frankincense	blue, yellow
moon glyph	jasmine, lotus, vanilla, sandalwood	silver, violet

continued

Symbol	Scents	Colors
solar wheel	nutmeg, orange, clove, tobacco	gold, orange
Mars glyph	basil, cumin peppermint, ginger	red

CHAPTER 10

Astral Projection
Method 6: Stepping
Out of Your Dreams

In chapter 4, astral projection is defined as any state in which your consciousness is immersed in a different time or place from that of your physical body. By this definition, the act of dreaming is also a form of astral projection. It surprises many beginners to find that most regular astral travelers make little or no distinction between dreaming and astral projection—rather, they have discovered that harnessing the power of dreams can become an excellent conduit for controlled astral travel.

One much-publicized type of dream control is what is known as *lucid dreaming*, a state in which the dreamer is fully aware of dreaming, yet remains asleep and takes control of the dream's content, shaping its direction. Once this is achieved, all worlds, time, and places are open to you; this fact is what makes lucid dreaming an act of astral projection.

The term "lucid dreaming" was coined in the late 1960s by psychologist and sleep researcher Frederik van Eeden, and has never been discarded. Books on the subject have enjoyed peaks and valleys of popularity over the past two decades, though there remains some confusion over what the term really means.

Lucid dreaming actually refers to a condition in which you recognize that you are dreaming *while* you are dreaming and, instead of waking, you remain asleep to take charge of your actions and reactions. Someone in the middle of a lucid dream may even leave the current dreamscape and travel elsewhere to complete the dream. Therefore, in all the ways that count, the dream actually becomes an inner world experience that is just like an astral projection. Lucid dreaming is not the same thing as dream control.

Dream control may occur whether or not the dreamer is consciously aware of dreaming. Though the dreamer may have fallen asleep with a conscious plan to dream about a certain subject, and though they may in fact follow through and actually *have* a dream about that subject, the dreamer will have little or no control over the details and direction of the dream. Therefore, the *control* in "dream control" refers to control over deciding on the subject of a dream, not over its content and storyline. Very young adults are good at gaining this type of non-lucid control, though they regrettably lose this ability as they enter their mid-teens—years when society teaches them to leave the fantasy world of adolescence behind and learn to focus on the "reality" of preparing for their future.

I'm very fond of lucid dreaming as a launch pad into astral projection. I've found virtually no difference between the two experiences. I learned to dream lucidly several years before I learned to consciously astral project, but it took several years more for me to understand how the two connect. I was having a good time, but I was not doing all that I could do with the skill. During my first few lucid experiences, I tended to allow the laws of physical reality to govern the dreams. Once I recognized that my lucid dreams were really astral adventures, I discovered that I was able to break those rules. I could fly, travel into fantasy realms, or seek out life in other worlds. In lucid dreams, I was every bit as unbounded by the earth plane as when astral projecting.

To make this method of astral projection work for you, you must first be able to recognize you are having a dream while it is occurring. That means you have to know without hesitation that you dream every night. Some people insist they never dream, and even seem proud of that fact. I'm sorry to have to tell them this is just not true. Not only do all humans dream, all mammals dream. Dreams appear as part of the natural sleep patterns we all follow. During the course of an average eight-hour night, human beings enter dream sleep up to six times. This means you have up to six times in the average night to recognize the fact that you're dreaming. When we first fall asleep, we progress rapidly to the delta (or deepest) level of sleep, and remain there for up to two hours. This initial delta phase constitutes the longest period of deep-level sleep we have for the night. Then our brains move up through the theta level and into the alpha, our lightest sleep state. This first alpha period is the shortest alpha period of the night. As the hours pass and we continue to move up and down these cycles, the deepest sleep periods become shorter and the lighter ones longer.

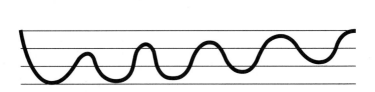

Figure 8. Sleep Cycle Pattern of a Normal Night

It is during these lightest sleep periods that we dream. Dream sleep is referred to as *REM* sleep, an acronym for Rapid Eye Movement. Under our closed eye lids our eyeballs are active, moving quickly from side to side as we "watch" our dreams unfold. Respiration increases, muscles twitch, and sometimes blood pressure rises. During REM sleep periods the voluntary muscles of our bodies become paralyzed by a chemical released by our brains. This is a protection mechanism built into mammals to prevent us from rising to physically act out our dreams.

Most of us have seen our pets in this state. They groan or growl, their paws twitching as if they are trying to run, yet they cannot because their bodies are paralyzed.

Several years ago I read about a sleep researcher who gave a cat a drug that blocked the chemical producing paralysis. When the cat dreamed, it got up and, with its eyes still closed, acted out what it was dreaming.

Researchers are not yet sure just what it is that triggers activation of the chemical that paralyzes us, but it may have something to do with the rapid, involuntary motion of the eyes. The simple act of being in an alpha state of mind is not enough. The paralyzing chemical is not released by those who meditate, even by those who are able to meditate deeply for prolonged periods. People who get deeply involved in guided meditation, a state which can mimic the dream state, also do not become paralyzed.

Like other astral travelers, lucid dreamers are often aware of both their astral and physical selves simultaneously, and a few report being aware of their paralysis. Many find it a disturbing sensation since it is unlike anything else they have experienced during other altered state exercises. Some are even distracted from their lucidity as the brain tries to cope with fear reactions, sometimes with bizarre results.

Someone once told me that, during lucid dreaming, he believed that demons were rendering him immobile and trying to possess his body. Once he was made aware that this was a perfectly natural occurrence during REM sleep, the demonic hallucinations stopped and he was able to enjoy his new skill.

If this dual awareness happens to you, just know that it's a natural part of dreaming. Nothing is trying to take control of your body, possess you, or invade you. The best thing to do in this situation is to mentally let go of the physical and try to focus on the dream state as a springboard to astral projection.

Even if you decide that you prefer other methods of astral projection to this one, the ability to have lucid dreams has other benefits. Lucid dreaming is therapeutic. It is a controlled dream state that allows you to work through problems using several different solutions. It can help you confront and overcome the terrors of night-mares and any recurring dreams that are disturbing.

Increasing Your Dream Awareness

Now that we've established that all of us dream, the next step is to remember having dreamed. If you cannot recall having had at least one dream per night after you wake, you will need to dramatically increase your awareness. Note that I didn't say you need to increase your dream recall capabilities—just your awareness. These are two different concepts.

As with dream recall, a dream diary works best to help jog nocturnal memories on waking. Many people hate the idea of working with a dream diary, so much so that I can actually hear the groans as I write this. But since we're aiming for awareness and not total recall, the way in which we will employ the dream diary is much less stringent.

Faithfully recording as many of the dream details as you can will swiftly increase your recall; unfortunately, it will also interrupt you during the periods that you're try-ing to become lucid. I've kept several dream diaries in my life and have found that, after several months, I'm awakened up to six times a night with vivid dream mem-ories to record.

This waking-at-all-hours method of detailed record-keeping has its advantages if your goal is prophetic dreaming or past-life recall, but to achieve lucid dreaming, you only need to be aware that you've dreamed at *some* point during the night.

All you need to do is make a record of your dream after you naturally wake in the morning. You don't even need to relate all the details, just a few points so that you are aware that a dream took place. When you get really carried away with the details of your dream diary, you tend to wake in the middle of dreams. This is a problem, since what you want is to recognize the fact that you're dreaming but to remain asleep so that you can take control of the dream content.

Another popular method of dream recall, which is not recommended as conducive to lucid dreaming, is setting alarms at intervals throughout the night. This is a hit and miss method that relies on catching you in a period of dream sleep that you will remember. Again, this will only condition you to *wake* during dreams rather than to recognize them.

Learning to Recognize the Dream State

To recognize that you're dreaming *while* you're dreaming, you have to fool the conscious mind into using its strongest capability—analytical reasoning. You have to bring this element into the process by making your mind constantly question whether you are dreaming or awake. Cuing yourself to ask this question using physical world triggers is the method most often suggested in books and articles on lucid dreaming. For example, every time you eat something, or pass through a gateway or threshold, or stop at a street light, you are to ask yourself, "Am I dreaming?"

I agree that to practice cuing yourself like this while still awake is a good idea, but I've found that unless you have very predictable dream sequences, selecting random physical world cues is not very productive. The dreams most of us remember are the ones with the strongest emotional content, not the ones in which we're engaged in mundane activities. Better to use cues that will get your attention whether asleep or awake.

Try cuing yourself to ask if you're dreaming anytime you hear something unbelievable or something startling, or when something happens to make you very happy or very sad. This can be as simple as hearing about a new policy at work you find incomprehensible, or watching a news program with shocking headlines.

Disbelief is a strong emotion that can echo throughout your entire system, engaging every part of you in the effort to find balance again. It echoes through your emotional body, which is what your astral self is made of. Strong emotions are themes in which both your conscious and subconscious minds will show interest, and the impact they have on your entire being will carry over into your dream world much better.

When I was hunting for good emotional cues, I found that I could work from *within* the dream. I often dreamed about family members who had died—during the dreams, I often felt disquieted. I knew that something was wrong. These people are no longer living; I shouldn't be able to interact with them in what appeared to be everyday reality to my dreaming mind. Sometimes I felt that I was mourning and interacting all at once. It was unpleasant.

After some effort I was able to ask the "Am I dreaming?" question, answer it, and take charge of the dreams. The key to making this work was my emotional state. I was aware of both the sense of joy at seeing these family members and of the knowledge that something in the joy was not right, and that an underlying current of grief was tugging me toward sadness at the same time.

Another way to enter the lucid dream state is by awakening from a dream but, instead of coming to full consciousness, to simply roll over and will yourself back into the dream by taking control. Do this by deciding quickly what action you want to take in the dream, then mentally see yourself doing it just as you would if you were practicing guided meditation (see chapter 8). This technique has always worked well for me. Due to a chronic illness, I'm a light sleeper and don't fall into the delta levels very often. I once managed to spend five entire hours in astral projection using this method.

According to Dr. Stephen LaBarge, author of *Lucid Dreaming* (Ballantine Books, 1986), only about ten percent of lucid dreams occur this way, but my experience and talking with others has shown the rate to be at least double that. This may be because my conversations usually involve persons who have followed occult paths and mystery religions for some time and are conditioned to making these inner world exercises work for them. In any case, it's worth the effort to see how it works for you.

If you're not someone who normally falls asleep with ease, you can allow your mind to flow into a controlled dream state using guided meditation. Allow the images to play in your head like a movie as you fall asleep. They should continue into the sleep state or be easily grasped again when you reach your first REM cycle. Plan to focus your mental energy on something you can be very involved with. Indulge in your most beloved fantasy. It doesn't have to, and probably shouldn't, be well-planned in advance. Simply have a general idea of what you want to imagine.

Young people are very adept at this method of lucid dreaming, and many are able to achieve enviably clear astral experiences this way. This may be because they have rich fantasy lives and are still young enough to have every possible road in life still open to them; and the inner world scenarios with which they can become involved are endless.

If you are in your twenties or beyond, look back and see if you can remember a time in your life when such things occurred naturally while you were alone in bed and only half asleep. This half-sleep state is called the *hypnogogic* state: a fluid period during which your mind is highly suggestible, especially if you're young. Chances are, you engaged in this activity to some extent once upon a time, though you probably did not recognize it for what it is.

There are several devices on the market that are purported to help you know when you enter REM sleep. They use the same methods that sleep labs have used to document the lucid dreaming phenomenon, measuring body relaxation, brain activity, respiration and blood pressure levels and, most importantly, eye movements. They alert you either by light signals or sounds, and some people report that they work very well. If you choose to use one of these (see the Appendix for the address of the Lucidity Institute, which sells them), be careful that you don't allow them to become a crutch without which you cannot function. You want to be able to independently recognize your dream states so that you can use them anywhere, anytime, as a springboard into the astral world.

Once you can answer that central question, "Am I dreaming?" in the affirmative, allow yourself to take control and go where you want to go. This *is* astral projection; it is a state that should last until you either wake up or fall back into a theta level of sleep again. You will not be harmed by this natural recession into deeper sleep. You may even find that your next cycle of REM dream sleep will allow you to continue on your astral journey from right where you left off.

Some teachers of lucid dreaming ask you to focus on a particular image in order to trigger an awareness of dreaming. This was made popular recently through the writings of Carlos Casteneda concerning his apprenticeship to Yacqui spiritual teacher Don Juan. In this case, Carlos was asked to try to hold his hands up in front of his face while he was dreaming, and to then "see" them. At that point he would become lucid.

I've known several people who swear that this method of dream recognition works for them, but I have found it to be exceptionally difficult. In my opinion, if you are conscious enough of your dream state to remember to look at a specific object, you're lucid enough to astral project.

If you want to try this method, I recommend that you select an object to look at that is always present, such as a hand, foot, or leg. Tell yourself that if you see your own hand or other body part, you'll realize that you are dreaming. You can attempt to ensure that you see your chosen body part by telling yourself before you go to sleep that you are going to do so.

The Lucid Dream
Astral Projection Process

Unlike the previous methods in this book, which tell you to seek out your designated private place to astral project, this method works best during the course of your regular night's sleep. You should still make whatever special preparations you wish beforehand: undress or wear nightclothes, don a talisman (as long as it is not one that goes around your neck!), turn on some gentle music, turn up the heat to keep yourself warm, etc., but avoid lighting fires or setting anything in motion that you cannot control during an entire night's sleep.

If you have elected to use a form of guided meditation (such as personal fantasy) as a way to ease yourself into the lucid state, it is best if you go to bed at least an hour earlier than usual so that you are not too tired to put your energy into the scenario you wish to view.

Lie down on your back, arms either loose at your side or raised over your head. These are positions in which the shamans of many cultures have used to enter sacred sleep; they seem to be conducive to opening us up to the other worlds. Avoid lying on your side or stomach while you are still learning, since these postures tend to be associated by us with dead-to-the-world sleep states that are not inviting to psychic experiences. Avoid placing your hands and arms over your stomach or chest area, as this may set up the same tensions as crossing your arms or legs would in a sitting position. Some people also believe that doing this will impede the flow of energy to and from your chakras.

Take a few moments to make sure that you are as comfortable as possible—at least comfortable enough to maintain this position until you fall into a deep, non-dream sleep. If you're not comfortable, make any desired changes now. Then close your eyes and take a few deep, slow breaths. As you begin to release your physical tension, also release any negative thoughts, feelings, or intentions from your mind. With each breath, feel yourself relaxing and being freed from negative energies of any kind.

Continue to breathe slowly, making sure that every part of your physical self is fully relaxed. You want to allow your body to precede you into sleep while conditioning your mind to your chosen dream world. Beginners may have trouble not falling asleep immediately once they are fully relaxed. Practice will help to extend the conscious period; so will going to bed a little earlier than usual.

If you're going to indulge in personal fantasy as a means of entering lucidity, allow the images to form now. Make them as real and engaging as possible. Allow your innermost desire to be seen on the movie screen in your mind.

If you are going to attempt to either 1) return to sleep after awakening from REM sleep, or 2) try to cue yourself while in REM sleep, then allow yourself to fall asleep naturally while mentally conditioning yourself with words and mental imagery to recognize the fact that you are dreaming when it begins, but to remain in the dream state rather than waking. Ask yourself if you're dreaming several times as you begin to fall asleep. In this hypnogogic state some dream images will occur, and this cuing will help you know what it feels like to recognize a dream. When you can answer your "Am I dreaming?" question in the affirmative, take charge by directing yourself to do whatever or go wherever you like.

Waking from REM sleep is fairly easy since it takes place during the lightest stages of sleep, and this can be exacerbated when you realize that you are dreaming for the first time. We have been conditioned since childhood to look at these inner world visions as "just dreams." We've been told that they're not real. We have, in many circumstances, been drilled to believe that waking is best if we know that we're dreaming, whether that dream is pleasant or nightmarish.

If the thrill of recognizing your dream state wakes you (as it did for me in the beginning), simply close your eyes and mentally take charge of your dream self. This may seem forced at first but, as your mind falls back into the deeper alpha levels, your dream state should fully kick in and, with luck, you can continue.

When you wake in the morning, you will likely find yourself again in the midst of REM sleep, unless it's one of those dreaded mornings when you must wake to an alarm clock. If you have the luxury of waking slowly, immediately try to project yourself into a dream state again. Your purpose is to either attempt lucid dreaming or to regain memories of dreams in which you achieved lucidity and astral projection but were only dimly aware of it.

As with usual dream experiences, astral experiences tend to feel unreal when you wake, and the details grow ever more hazy the longer we are awake. Record any lucid dream images or astral projection experiences in your astral journal immediately on waking to avoid losing the detail.

Tips and Suggestions for the Lucid Dreaming Astral Projection Method

This is one astral projection method that does not accept outside help easily. You will have only five or six chances during the course of an average eight-hour night to enter and recognize that you are in REM sleep—fewer chances if you sleep less. There is little you can do to increase your periods of REM sleep; and there are no herbal preparations that can help you recognize your dreams. Sometimes an incense that is known to help open sleepers to prophetic dreams (like jasmine or vervain) can help in terms of giving you more interesting dreams, but it will not assist with the all-important lucidity.

If insomnia is a chronic problem while you are trying to learn lucid dreaming, try using teas made from agrimony, valerian, or catnip. They have all been used as natural sleep inducers, although they do not increase REM sleep. These are certainly better for you than commercial sleeping pills, which should be avoided at all costs. Even the over-the-counter variety containing primarily diphenhydramine promotes an unnatural sleep that can significantly reduce REM time. Most of the prescription sleeping medicines, such as amitriptylene (which is actually an anti-depressant), are designed to give those who take them as much delta, or deep sleep, as possible. These will severely inhibit REM sleep, which is neither healthy nor conducive to your purposes.

For your best chance at REM sleep, try rearranging your personal schedule so that you get as much rest per night as your body requires to function properly. For most people, this is somewhere between six and nine hours. Within a week or so of falling into a regular sleeping pattern, you'll find that your REM sleep comes to you on a regular cycle. I'm aware that finding time to sleep eight hours a night is a problem. For most of us, life is just too busy to see to proper rest, and we try in vain to make up for it on weekends. If it is completely impossible for you to get enough sleep each night, try telling yourself to be more aware as the end of your sleep cycle approaches, since this is when you are likely to have the most recognizable REM experiences.

PART THREE

THE NEXT STEP

INTRODUCTION TO PART 3

Challenging the Boundaries

Time and space constrictions were placed on your mind by the society into which you were born, but fortunately they have no meaning in the astral world. Once the basic techniques of astral projection are mastered, you never again have to exist solely within the boundaries of what our enculturated brains perceive to be attainable.

In your astral body you can visit other countries or planets, other times and eras, and communicate with people and spirits who are physically far away from our everyday world. With the mastery of this skill will come the luxury of being "in two places at one time" whenever we need or desire. You may choose to travel to the bedside of sick loved ones and help heal their illnesses; read and understand your Akashic Records; enter the faery realm of the nature spirits; explore the kingdoms of the elements; reunite with the dead; make profound changes in your physical life; and attend classes on any subject you wish. Astral projection can also be a valuable tool for spiritual growth and self-understanding, since we learn on the astral plane both through our own explorations as well as with the assistance of guides and teachers whom we meet on our travels.

These final chapters will give you an overview of several practices that are usually easy for beginners to succeed at, and will provide you with the keys for beginning to explore them. Further assistance can be acquired by consulting the Appendix and Bibliography at the back of the book.

CHAPTER 11

Viewing Your
Akashic Records

Many spiritually inclined people wish to learn astral projection for one purpose only: to be able to view their Akashic Records. This is a laudable goal. It elevates astral projection from an exercise in "flying around and looking at things" to a spiritual art that can provide you with the self-understanding you need in order to grow.

The Akashic Records are a compendium of everything that has happened to every single soul from the time it was created until the present. The term comes from the

Hindustani word *akasha*, meaning spirit or soul. Psychologist C. G. Jung introduced us to the concept of a "collective unconscious," which in effect can be understood as an astral record of all past and future events, thoughts, actions, and intents. Experience has shown us that these records are catalogued by individual, so that any one person can look up the record of his or her own soul's eternal progression toward its goals.

Because the Akashic Records are no more than images that have been permanently impressed on the astral plane, the ways in which we can view them are only as limited as our imagination. The most common vision is to see the records as a giant book where we can read about our long past. Some see this book as part of a great astral library full of other soul books, others as a single book on an etheric pedestal in the middle of the astral. Some read the words from the books, and for others the book turns into a mirror in which past actions and events are played out in full detail.

My records have never appeared in book form to me; rather, they show themselves projected onto a wall, somewhat like the movie screen in a theater. Sometimes I'm there watching alone, but most of the time my spirit guide comes to sit with me, either of her own volition or at my request. Sometimes she even tells me that there are other records I should be looking at that would be more useful to me. Occasionally she offers commentary, but mostly she allows me to work things through on my own and doesn't say anything unless I ask direct questions.

You might also hear an audio version of your Akashic Records being played back to you with all the drama and commentary that you would expect from a well-produced radio play. I knew a woman once whose spirit guide would simply tell her in detail everything that she needed to know. An artist friend of mine views her records over the shoulder of an elven sketch artist who draws pictures on a large pad. As she watches, the drawings become animated and act out the events she is reviewing. Her principal spirit guide often stands with her, sometimes even coaching the sketch artist about the way something should appear.

A large part of your Akashic Records' appearance depends on how you want to view them and on the type of person you are. Very visual people will likely see the events played out like a movie; older people may find the radio play idea most comfortable; and younger people might find themselves in a high-tech room with multi-media possibilities.

Astral Ethics and the Akashic Records

The Akashic Records are probably the greatest single source of spiritual wisdom you will encounter in this lifetime, so you don't want to run the risk of losing the privilege to consult them as a result of misusing them. Remember that like-energies attract like-energies in the astral, and any underhanded intentions will rebound on you very quickly. If someone else's soul records need to be shown to you because that soul's life impacts on yours, the images will come to you as you need them. You will not have to snoop.

I've been privy to some unpleasant stories from people who ignored these warnings, and all were sorry. One person who admitted to seeking out records to determine whether or not his girlfriend was seeing another man found himself immediately surrounded by a goon squad of what he assumed were lower astral beings. They tried to prevent him from returning to his body—only the interference of his guide sent them on their way. The guide then showed him the proper way to find out about his problem without being privy to records that were none of his business. He was made to understand that his problem was a lack of faith in himself, not in her or their relationship.

Another person related an experience of how she was allowed to continue viewing the records of others for several months, all the while telling herself that she was just trying to better understand her friends and family. When she finally got back to her original goal of self-understanding she was rewarded with "horror movies" of wars, famines, and other atrocities, which may or may not have had anything to do with her own past. It was a long time before she could enter the astral again with comfort, and even longer before she could permit herself to look at her own Akashic Records again.

Some people have excellent psychic self-defense mechanisms in place, and these include barriers against astral intruders. You may find yourself up against one of their astral guard dogs if you trespass on their soul records.

The best way to judge the ethical qualities of any action on the astral is to ask yourself "How would I feel if someone was doing this to me?" Be honest when you answer this question.

Finding Your Akashic Records

No matter how hard you try to make your mind a blank, you are going to find that you have a lot of preconceived ideas about how the place where your Akashic Records are kept is going to look, as well as by which method or methods you are going to view them. There's nothing wrong with this; in fact, it's a helpful tool for getting you there the first time. After that, don't be surprised if the place and methods change or vary a great deal.

After you are used to astral projecting, you will be able to get to your records at any time during a projection. If you suddenly feel the need to take a look, moving yourself at will through the astral will be easy. As a beginner you might find it easier to astral project solely with this intent, conditioning your mind to this goal. To do this, as you start your astral projection process, keep in mind the ultimate goal of viewing your Akashic Records. You can do this with visualization or with a chant, or both if it helps. This helps condition all levels of your mind to the task and keeps you focused there. Once you are projected, either fly toward or will yourself to be in the vicinity of your records. If no image immediately comes to you, allow your preconceived notion to form the picture for you and work with that until another image appears.

At this point in the process your guide may appear to you, or you may wish to call on her or him for assistance. For many of us, viewing our Akashic Records for the first time is a very emotional experience. The first time I viewed mine, I asked about a very intense past-life issue that I had been grappling with for several months. The answers to the puzzle were shown to me on a movie screen. I immediately recognized my former self, but my consciousness remained with my astral self. My astral body was emotionally involved in the experience but was able to remain in control of its emotions. At the same time, I could feel the tears pouring down the face of my physical body, giving me the oddest sensation of being in two completely different places at once while being fully conscious of both. I was in emotional over-load in both worlds. My guide was a great help in sort-ing out the important issues and taking what was most useful from the experience while letting go of the rest.

Your first visit to your records may leave you with more questions than answers if you are unfocused about your precise intent. Here is where guidance is invaluable—your guide can help you to interpret what you find, show you where to get additional information about a particular issue, or take you to a place where you can view the records by a different method than the one you initially thought you would use.

The first time you view your records, it's best to know precisely what information you're after, and not overload your senses. I wanted to know everything about myself in one trip. Instead of settling the questions in my mind, the images all began to blur once I returned to the phys-ical. It was hard to sort out what was what, even though I was trying to record it all immediately in my journal. There's plenty of time to explore everything you wish, and no need to rush. Take your time to fully understand one aspect of yourself before taking on another.

As you approach the books, screen, library, or other means by which you will view your records, try to form in your mind a single issue or question you wish to explore. For beginners, the best practice is usually to say, "Please show me what will be most useful for me to know now." This allows the records or your guide to hone in on what is most important at the moment, and prevents you from taking on issues you might not be spiritually ready to handle. Suggestions for issues to explore initially are:

1. The purpose of your current incarnation.
2. Any past-life issue that you have been unable to resolve by other means.
3. The state of your spiritual progress.
4. A personal relationship issue.

Many who view their records on a regular basis like to create some sort of "astral residence" where they can be comfortable while they do this. Variations on this theme are found in the astral temple and the astral garden popular in other occult traditions. Remember that thought-forms live forever on the astral, and repeated building up of the imagery of your astral home will make it more and more real, and easier to get to and work in, each time you go there.

To create your astral residence, simply relax and begin to imagine what your ideal living place would be like. Create a home, room, and furnishings, then move outdoors and create landscape. Next time you astral project, mentally take yourself to a vacant space on the higher astral planes (or ask your guide to escort you to one), then mentally project these images outward and spend as much time as you need making them real. Don't be surprised if certain touches add themselves. Just like you can't control every aspect of a plot of ground you buy in the physical, you will have irregularities in the astral as well, and these are usually images that will prove useful to you later. Only instead of unwanted weeds in a garden, you may find other objects coming and going that are being put there either by your subconscious or your guide. For example, that candleholder that suddenly appears on your desk top may be there to illuminate your way home during an astral blackout.[1]

Be creative in designing and decorating your new home, but be sure to include in your residence a system for viewing the Akashic Records. This can be anything from a courier service to and from the astral library or a home movie screen and sound system that plays your past at your will. Whatever the means, it will always be there for you to view and study.

---

1. A point at which the light in the astral world appears to dissipate, leaving the traveler in darkness.

CHAPTER 12

Remote Healing

R*emote healing* is the art of performing metaphysical healing from a physical location away from that of the person asking for your help. Remote healing can be accomplished from both the physical world and the astral plane. The difference between the two techniques is that when one is remote healing from the physical plane, a ritual is enacted whose purpose is to send healing energy out to the person who has requested it. When healing from the astral plane, the healer actually astral projects to the physical location of the one in need.

Healing and Spiritual Ethics

It's hard to understand why healing someone without their permission is wrong, since the desired outcome seems so positive. But you must remember that what *you* see as a desirable solution to an illness might not be shared by your unwilling patient. Most newcomers to occult practices have trouble with the concept of free will.

In almost every spiritual system, there is an injunction for us to secure permission from the subject before any healing can be done. To proceed otherwise is a violation of free will. In many systems, such an infringement is believed to rebound on the one who trespasses, no matter how good the original intent.

Even if you operate outside the boundaries of any specific spiritual system, simple astral ethics should tell you what is right and wrong. How would you feel if someone else decided what was or was not going to be done for your own good, whether you liked it or not? Treat another's choices with the same respect that you wish your own to be treated with, and you'll likely not go wrong.

Healing works best when the energies of the ill person are engaged in the effort with you. This is another reason why that person's consent is important. If your intended subject is fighting you all the way—whether that person is even aware of putting up a struggle or not—you might as well not waste your time.

Advanced Art or Innate Talent?

I've heard it argued that remote healing is an advanced astral art. Others claim it's fairly simple, especially when compared to other astral practices. Some say healers are born with their gift, and it cannot be learned to any great degree, though most diligent people can learn the basics. What it all probably comes down to is whether or not you have any native talent as a healer. Healing has never been one of my strongest skills, and the extra effort it requires for me to do it successfully pushes me to classify it as a more advanced practice. Those who are innately gifted healers will probably find remote healing to be fairly easy once they have mastered the art of astral projection.

Another argument for it being a more advanced practice, or at least an intermediate one, is the fact that healing usually requires that at some point you absorb part or all of the illness being treated into yourself. This is eventually released and grounded, of course, but many long-time practitioners of remote healing feel this sudden intake of illness cannot be handled adequately by beginners, and that they, too, will become sick.

Those who are not gifted healers, but who have managed to teach themselves to be very proficient at the art, sometimes discover that they cannot find their way astrally to everyone who needs them. This underscores our basic understanding of astral projection as an exercise in manipulating the emotional body. If a strong emotional attachment to your astral goal is not present, then it can be very difficult to succeed. When the person who needs your help is someone you know and love, and who trusts you to help, the process will always be easier.

Only you can weigh all of these considerations against what you know of your own skills and affinities, and only you can decide whether or not to attempt healing through astral projection. Naturally, you will improve with practice, just like the real pros in this art did. They were beginners once, just like you.

The Mechanics of Remote Healing

We are going to cover only the astral plane method of remote healing here—the one requiring that the healer astral project to the physical location of the subject—since astral projection is our focus. You should be aware that if you have skimped on working with the chakra cleansing and balancing exercises (chapter 2), you will have trouble with remote healing. Much of it is based on cleansing and balancing the chakra centers of others. If you don't feel up to speed on this, go back now and review the steps.

While in your astral consciousness, you are better able to see things that are usually hidden to your physical eyes. Many new astral travelers are surprised to learn that illness can actually be seen on the auric field or astral body surrounding someone's physical self.

As you approach the subject, allow your inner awareness to be wide open to impressions. The first thing you are likely to notice is dark patches on their aura. Allow your eyes to roam over the entire body, hunting for patterns to these dark spots. You may notice that they either cluster at the site of the illness (for instance, over the lungs for a lung disease, or over the stomach for a stomach disorder) or near one or two specific chakras associated with that area. Sometimes you may notice that they are at both places. Mentally take note of these spots so that you can give them extra attention later in the healing process.

Next, run your astral hands through the aura of the person to be healed. Keep them no more than two inches from the physical body at all times. Try to sense any irregularities in the magnetic field—places where it seems exceptionally thin or thick, or where you feel a magnetic field pushing back. These are spots that may indicate further illness in the body.

Make another pass over the body with your astral hands, only this time visualize a balancing energy coming from them that will restore the aura to its balanced state and repair all tears, weak spots, or surges in the field. You can visualize this energy being drawn into you from any positive place in the astral, or from the divine world above you. Do not use and deplete your own energy in this procedure. Balancing energy should be drawn into you and then distributed.

When you are satisfied that this is done, turn your attention to the chakras—especially the ones you noted earlier that contained dark patches. Balance all of the chakras, from the root to the crown, by projecting a balancing energy into them. You can allow this to flow into you and then out through your astral hands or you can mentally will it to be there. I usually see this energy projecting like a beacon of light from my forehead. Make each chakra clean and vivid in color (see *Color Associations for Chakras*, page 32), and see each one pulsating with unimpeded energy flow. As you come to the chakras that have dark patches, either sift the patches out with your astral hands and save them to be grounded later, or mentally will them to dissipate under the heat of the healing energy you are projecting into the chakra.

Healing with Color

The art of healing with color is a study unto itself, and if you want to pursue remote healing you will find the effort worthwhile. You can find most of what you need to begin in a slender and inexpensive book by Ted Andrews called *How to Heal With Color* (Llewellyn, 1992). You might also look in Evelyn M. Monahan's *The Miracle of Metaphysical Healing* (Reward Books, 1977).

To transmit color energy astrally, the easiest and safest method is to draw the energy into yourself from the astral world around you, and then to project it into the patient through touch. Remember that it is better to err on the side of caution when using color energy. Don't overdo it. It's better to use a little each day than to overload someone with a single energy all at once.

In general, brown and green are considered to balance and heal almost anything. Red and orange provide energy, but they can raise blood pressure too. White, silver, or gold are neutral in terms of healing energy, and are the best to use if you are uncertain about the exact color needed. A list of suggested colors for healing follows, and should be used as a guideline only, not as a carved-in-stone prescription.

Healing Characteristics of Color

Color	Characteristics
red	stimulates all systems; increases heart rate and elevates blood pressure; useful for assistance in weight loss and blood diseases; good for treating hypothermia due to its tendency to increase heat; never to be used on a fever; helps burn down tumors
orange	stimulates the central nervous system; aids in ailments of the digestive tract and respiratory system
yellow	purifies blood; has positive effect on mental outlook; eases upset stomach
green	causes growth and regeneration (so it should never be used on a suspected tumor); good choice for heart ailments; this is a neutral healing color that neither overstimulates nor causes heating of the body; also good for healing sick plants; calms and soothes
blue	soothes nervous systems; lowers blood pressure; induces peaceful sleep; good for many childhood diseases—sore throats, toothaches, tonsillitis and strep throat; works as an aid to antiseptics; helps lower fever

continued

Color	Characteristics
purple	good for easing very serious illnesses; eye and ear disorders; helps heal broken bones; helps balance the emotional body; helps heal surgical scars
brown	good choice for healing all manner of illnesses in animals; this is a neutral color that can be used when you are unsure of the best color for the problem; helps ground someone who is unfocused about what medical treatment to use

Many remote healers recommend that you end each session by surrounding the patient with a protective egg of white light. They say that this strengthens the healing process, rebalances any systems that you were not fully able to mend, and helps protect the patient from new germs or viruses that may be waiting to invade the weakened system.

Before you end the healing session and prepare to return home, look around the area where the person is resting. You may see vague shapes of other beings in the vicinity. Some might be loving presences, but others will clearly be malevolent—either the spirit manifestation of the illness or another negative entity that has attached itself to the person, inhibiting the healing process.

Feel free to dismiss these beings, by force if necessary. Ordering their retreat or sending a blast of positive light from your astral self to the beings often works. If the beings do not respond to you, call on either your guide or the guide of the person you are healing to assist you by mentally requesting their presence.

When all malevolent beings are banished, and the aura and chakras of the ill person have been balanced, seal your healing efforts with an egg of protective gold-white light. You may transfer that light to the person by any of the means already mentioned. This act not only offers a final balancing energy to the effort, but also acts as a temporary psychic barrier to the malevolent beings so that the immune system can be strengthened.

When you have completed this process, return to your body, awaken as usual, and then be sure to ground any excess energy that you might have picked up. You can use the same method as you used to ground your Body of Light (page 101). This is exceptionally important in this case, since that excess may contain vestiges of illness. You will want to rid yourself of it as soon as possible.

Like other forms of healing, remote healing is usually not a one-treatment-cures-all event, and you may need to repeat your efforts on successive occasions until you are satisfied that you've done all you can.

Using All Your Resources

The best thing you can do for anyone who comes to you for healing is to not only provide remote healing, but to refer them to a licensed physician for conventional treatment as well. Metaphysical healing works best in conjunction with medical science, and it keeps you from being charged with practicing medicine without a license. It also brings us into compliance with the occult law telling us we must back up our astral efforts in the physical world in order to be successful.

The number of doctors open to including holistic medicine—including various metaphysical treatments, nutri-
tional support, herbal supplements, and visualization—is
still small, but growing. With a little effort, a physician
who is able to treat the whole person can be found. This
will benefit your remote healing efforts as well.

Keeping "Medical" Records

Because people respond to different techniques, it is
essential that you keep excellent records of exactly what
you do in each session of remote healing. This will help
you to achieve a necessary understanding of your own
strengths and weaknesses, and the person you have
been asked to help will have a right to know exactly
what has been done on his or her behalf.

Sometimes, if you're healing a person who is skilled at
astral projection, they will be able to assist you when you
come to them in astral form. This always helps to put
your energy in just the right place, and it's nice when the
person you're helping can actually remember the session.

You don't ever want to be accused of practicing medicine without a license, so it's always wise to document
what you do and don't do, making it clear that this was all
done with *remote* healing; you never prescribed any concrete form of treatment or physically touched another person in any way. Be sure to note that you have asked the
person you're helping to seek qualified medical help in
addition to and in support of your own work. Finally, as a
precaution in our litigation-happy society, you may want
to ask the person you're healing to sign a formal agree-
ment, stating that he or she understands that what you're
doing is intended to be supported by orthodox medicine.

CHAPTER 13

Creative Visualization

Creative visualization is the practice of mentally envisioning a desired outcome, infusing it with personal energy, and then releasing it to the cosmos so that it can grow to manifest in the physical. While all that sounds unduly complicated, what it boils down to is that it creates a thoughtform on the astral plane that, with proper effort, can be brought into the physical world.

The advantage of engaging in creative visualization within the astral world is self-evident. This is, after all, where visualizations must first take form. It makes sense to create them on their own turf. Visualization also allows you to step outside of the "head world" of the process, and watch as your deepest desire literally manifests before your eyes. In the astral, you can even allow yourself to be a part of the visualization, making yourself the star of the visualization "movie." This form of participation feeds energy into the scene that links it intimately with you, making the visualization easier to manifest.

The terms *creative visualization* and *positive magic* are sometimes used interchangeably, depending on the spiritual orientation of the one doing the visualizing. In both cases, the goal is to take a desired need and bring it into being. Both terms refer to more than just thinking about something; they imply a process that seeks to attain that "something" by efforts in both the seen and unseen worlds.

Creative visualization is easy, though I've had many people tell me that they simply cannot do it. Their insistence that this is a skill beyond them is probably due to misconceptions about the process. Too many people make it harder than it really is. Visualization is mental vision. You visualize each time you daydream, work out a project in your head, create a new decorating scheme for your house, draw and paint, or plan a vacation. Any time you think about something and see it happening, you are visualizing. What makes it *creative* visualization is the level at which you control the process and the energy you invest in making your thoughts a reality.

People who think they cannot visualize usually try to create mental images that are much more complex than needed. The visualizations you create do not have to appear as if they came from the camera of a professional photographer or cinematographer. They can be still, animated, or a combination, and they do not need to be three-dimensional. They can be seen as sketches, vignettes, or they may even be non-visual. Some people who are not visually oriented "hear" their visualizations while they sense the scene's emotional impact. It's the emotional aspect you attach to your visualization that will provide its power.

Energizing Your Desires

Before astral projecting for the purpose of creative visualization, take as much time as you need to assess your desire. Occult wisdom teaches us that your desire has the greatest chance of manifesting if it is also something that you really need. In other words, you will have trouble manifesting a million dollars just because you want it, though getting enough cash to pay next month's rent is well within your creative grasp.

You should also plan how to back up your astral efforts on the physical plane. This is another bit of wisdom that those involved with the occult have always known: *your astral efforts work best if backed up by action in the physical world.* For example, if you are visualizing a healing, it isn't enough just to imagine. You also need to go to the doctor and take care of yourself, participating in the process on every level of your being.

This idea underscores the occultist's belief in the microcosm, or self, as a reflection of the macrocosm, or the whole. What affects one eventually affects the other, so in order to make them both work for you, you have to make efforts in both realms.

Give some thought ahead of time to precisely how you wish to visualize your outcome. This is important no matter on which plane of existence you are focusing your efforts. You want to make sure your final outcome is:

1. What you really need and want.

2. Not harmful to others.

3. Not a tool to take from others in order that you might receive.

4. Indicative of a goal that you are emotionally attached to, to a degree that will keep you working for it until it is achieved.

5. Indicative of a goal that you are willing to devote both astral world and physical world efforts to in order to achieve.

Sometimes using a divination device like tarot cards or rune stones, or some quality meditation time, can help bring some or all of these aspects into focus for you. Ask your chosen divination tool for an overview of your desire. Take notes, then ask it to show you the probable outcome of your having what you want. Again take notes, and spend at least twenty-four hours thinking over your choices. Make any amendments to your goal that you want, then try the divination process again.

If you do not have a divination device to rely on, or you'd just rather not use it at this time, try spending time in general meditation focusing on your goal and all of its ramifications (refer back to chapter 1 if you need to). Do this for several consecutive nights, and be sure to make a note of the impressions that come to you—both during the meditation and in your dreams.

The Path of Least Resistance

If you're repeatedly having trouble making creative visualization work for you, you may be creating too much mental detail. One aspect of the process often cautioned to beginners is the sequence, or point in time, that you pick for your visualization. This is not just another caution to keep your visualizations in the present tense, which you should be doing automatically by this time; it simply means you need to be sure that you're visualizing yourself actively *enjoying* what you desire, not trying to visualize how it will come to you.

Creative visualization follows the laws of any other type of energy. Energy is always in motion, and it always takes the path of least resistance. The visualization you hope to manifest should be allowed to manifest in the way that is easiest for it to do so, without harming anyone else. In your visualizations, it is best to see yourself enjoying the benefits of what you desire as if it is already a part of your life. Don't try to dictate how it will come about. In doing this, you may either be asking for a sequence of events that would hurt or take away from someone else or that does not reflect the easiest manner for your desire to manifest, or both.

The consequences of harming others for your own gain is obviously bad enough, but you should also remember that when you toss a roadblock in the path of least resistance, you could be delaying the achievement of your goal or keeping it permanently out of reach.

The time you spend planning any occult operation is considered by experienced occultists to mark the beginning of your efforts. The beginning is *not* the point at which you finally put the plan into action, so don't feel like you're wasting your time in this planning stage. The very act of thinking is magical in nature. It causes change to occur. All things that have manifested in the physical world were once no more than an idea in someone's mind: a thoughtform that was given energy, backed up in the physical, and then birthed into being.

You should be aware that as things change in both the astral and physical worlds, you will have to adapt your visualizations accordingly. You won't be able to plan for every eventuality. The time you invest in the planning stage will open your creative psyche. As a result, many potential problems will be avoided before they even have a chance to appear. Furthermore, you will be better equipped to deal with those problems that do show up.

When you have a plan for your creative visualization, and a scheme to back it up in the physical world, it is time to begin your creative visualization on the astral plane. To do this you first must enter the astral plane by whatever method is easiest for you. For this effort you might find that using a guided meditation connected to your goal works well, but any other method that works for you is just as good.

The Astral Creative Visualization Process

Once you are floating free on the astral plane, allow yourself to be taken to an area where there is nothingness. It may appear to you in one of several forms: like an area of dense fog, or as an eternal blackness, or even as a blank cyclorama-like enclosure onto which you can project your mental imagery.

Unless you are very uncomfortable with what appears, assume that you have arrived at the best place for your creative visualization work. If you don't like where you find yourself, either travel on until you find somewhere to your liking, or ask your guide to escort you to an appropriate place. This will be the place where you will begin painting the canvas of your imagination.

Using the plans you made as your blueprint, begin building your inner vision, making changes if and where necessary. You can do this by seeing yourself from a remote position enjoying your desire, or you can step into the scene you're building and experience it from a first-person point of view. I recommend the latter, since it will give you more emotional involvement in your visualization. This not only strengthens the effort, but will let you know if something is not right about the scene, in which case you might want to step out and rethink your goal.

When you have built up the scene as clearly as you can using whatever method works best for you, freeze the scene (or words, or emotions, etc.) in your mind and energize it by one of the following methods:

1. Draw energy into your astral self by taking it from the astral world around you. Then project it into the image you have created by using more mental imagery. See the image vibrate with a new intensity as you feed it the power through which it can manifest.

2. Mentally make the image into a 360-degree wall surrounding you. Once you are in the middle of it, allow your astral self to fuse with the imagery, making the two of you one being. Hold this image for several minutes, feeling yourself fully a part of your desire before you allow the image to separate from you again.

3. Mentally project energy into a color that you feel corresponds to your desire, and allow it to form an egg around the created image. Allow the egg to begin to blend into the image so that it infuses the entire scene. After you have infused the image with the color energy, allow it to return to normal. A list of suggested color correspondences follows:

Color Associations for Creative Visualization

Color	**Corresponding Issues**
red	passion, anger, action, sex
orange	friendship, attraction, action with thought, employment
yellow	intellectual matters, school, teaching, study
green	matters of environment, money, growth, material acquisition, issues of the faery kingdom, fertility
blue	health, peace, sleep, tranquility, spiritual growth, clairvoyance, contact with spirits

violet	healing, serious health problems, connecting with the higher self, occult matters and skills
brown	home, land, animals and livestock, children
pink	peaceful home life, romantic love
silver	spiritual matters, connecting with the Goddess or other lunar deities, those things that are hidden
gold	investment, spiritual action, connecting with the God or other solar deities, those things that are apparent but not readily understood

4. Mentally project a rope of etheric energy flowing from your navel region into the heart of the image. Spend a few minutes experiencing the sensation of energy exchange between yourself and the picture of your desire so that you become a part of it and it becomes a part of you.

After you have energized the visualization, send it out into the universe to work on manifesting while keeping it linked to you through a tie that you create. Methods of linking might be:

1. To see a thread going from your visualization to one of your chakras.

2. To make a drawing of the visualization after
   you wake.

3. To make a talisman (instructions follow) that
   will help to draw in your desire.

You can use any number, including all, of these methods at once, or you may prefer to use just one. Do what
you feel works best for you—whatever will recall the
goal most clearly to your conscious mind at various
times during your waking life.

Making and Using a Talisman

Making a talisman for almost any need is fairly simple,
though they can become very complex in some occult
systems. A talisman is an object that is usually made by
the one who will be using it. It is empowered with personal energy that is focused on the goal of attracting a
certain item or condition.

My favorite kinds of talismans are small sections of colored cloth (refer to the color correspondences given earlier in this chapter for suggestions) into which items
relating to or reflecting the need are placed. For instance,
if you are doing creative visualization to help you get into
a certain college, you might choose yellow cloth for matters of study and place inside it pictures of the campus, a
corner torn from the school's catalog, a stone from the
grounds of the campus, and/or some written statements
of your goal. Visualize your desire as you make this, and
empower it in the same way you empowered your visualization in the astral. Keep the talisman with you until
you reach your goal, at which time it should be buried or
burned to release the energy flow you've created.

Creative Visualization:
Once is Never Enough

Let's face facts. If creative visualization was easy and fast, we'd all be doing it all the time. Every night all 5.5 billion of us would invade the astral plane with our desires, and we'd all return a few hours later rich, famous, and beautiful. Creative visualization is a powerful tool for success, as anyone who regularly practices it will tell you. But it's not a magic bullet that you shoot into a target to see instant results. It works best when you can remain committed to your goal over the long term, during which you repeat your creative visualization exercise as needed.

Some people will repeat their astral visualizations nightly, others will do it every few days or even once a week. The timing is up to you, and the schedule you set may vary according to your personal schedule, your physical world efforts, and the nature of the desire. The more energy you feed your goal, the better chance it will have of manifesting.

Shutting Down
the Creative Visualization Process

As we discussed in relation to the Body of Light in chapter 5, we are responsible for any and all astral images we create for the full duration of their existence. The word *creative* in "creative visualization" separates this operation from simple daydreaming. It describes an act of creation on the astral plane. You are making something very real—you must be aware of your creation while it exists and be ready to dismantle it when your need for it is over.

To stop the creative visualization energies when they are no longer needed or wanted, astral project to the place on the astral plane where you have built the image. Sever your connection to the image by using a knife to cut whatever energy flow you have set up between it and you. Mentally see the ends of the strings wither as they are cut. If the created image is still animated, shut it off. Freeze the image and begin to take it apart piece by piece. Take out major parts of it and see them break apart, but do not ground their energy. Simply see them become neutral energy patterns without programming, and allow them to be reabsorbed into the astral world so that you can draw on them later if you wish.

Creative Problem Solving on the Astral Plane

Creative visualization on the astral plane is an excellent method for creative problem solving and for energizing the outcome that you've discovered works best for you. Go to the place where you conduct creative visualizations, and this time, visualize the scene of your problem. Animate it and allow it to work itself through from beginning to end with you actively involved. You want to be as "into" the scene as possible so that you can assess your feelings about the success or failure of the solution. If you stand back, detached from it, you may decide a solution is right that would have felt wrong if you had allowed yourself to experience it rather than just watch.

If your first solution is unsatisfactory, allow the image to dissolve and flow down into the astral "earth" below you. Create the scene of the problem again and allow it work itself through with a new solution.

Keep going until you find a solution to your problem that works. Once you are satisfied with your outcome, you can either empower the image as you did your other creative visualizations, or you can simply take the answers back to the physical world with you and put them into action there.

Summary Statements

As these final chapters have shown you—or perhaps enticed you—an unlimited universe awaits the one who takes that first step toward conquering the astral plane. As we have seen, the steps to astral projection success are threefold:

1. Preparation for and understanding of the goal.

2. Experimentation with various projection methods and aids to discover which are most comfortable and workable.

3. Persistence.

Only you can provide the latter prerequisite, which is probably the most important one of all. One day, when you least expect it, you will discover your consciousness to be outside yourself, free of the constraints of your physical self, and soaring through this world and others at your will.

The unlimited universe is both inside and outside of yourself. It awaits your decision to challenge the boundaries of the ordinary and explore.

PART FOUR

RESOURCES
AND REFERENCES

Appendix

Your best chance of getting a response when contacting any of the businesses listed here is by including either an SASE (self-addressed stamped envelope) or an IRC (international reply coupon, to be used if you are addressing mail outside your own country) with your requests for information.

You should of course be aware that vendors can go out of business and magazines can go out of print for either financial or personal reasons. If you fail to get a response to your queries in a reasonable amount of time, you might try checking with directory assistance to get a phone number, or try calling the better business bureau in the respective area.

Some of the organizations listed have a site on the World Wide Web that will offer more information and will likely sell products. Since cyberspace addresses tend to change often and quickly, they have been omitted from this appendix. Use your computer's search engines to locate current URLs (Universal Resource Locators).

All contact information in this listing was updated a few months prior to publication, but if you are reading this book more than two years from its first printing, it may be wise to double check addresses first before doing any mailing.

Abyss
RR #1, Box 213 F
Chester, MA 01011
(413) 623-2155

Everything occult or magical you that ever wanted can be found at Abyss. Request their free catalog.

Balefire
6504 Vista Ave.
Wauwatosa, WI 53213

Balefire is a mail-order company that carries a large stock of oils and incenses that are designed for specific needs, including astral projection.

Co-op Essentials
5364 Ehlich Rd., Suite 402
Tampa, FL 33625

Co-op Essentials sells fine essential oils. Send $1.00 for their most current price list.

Dream Network
P.O. Box 1026
Moab, UT 84531
(801) 461-9003

Dream Network publishes the *Quarterly Journal Exploring Dreams and Myths*. It contains information on the relationship between dreams and astral projection. They also publish and sell a booklet entitled *The Art of Dreamsharing and Developing Dream Groups.* Write with SASE for subscription information.

Dreaming Spirit
P.O. Box 4263
Danbury, CT 06813-4263

Dreaming Spirit provides natural, homemade incenses, resins, oils, and tools for using them. They welcome inquiries about custom blends of incenses or oils. The $2.00 for their catalog is refundable with your first order.

I.I.P.C.
Rua Visconde de Piraj, 572
6 andar
Rio de Janeiro, RJ 22410-002
Brazil
(55) 21-512-9229
E-mail: iipc@ax.apc.org

The International Institute of Projectiology and Conscientiology (I.I.P.C.) is non-profit research and education organization. It has offices and classes worldwide, including in the United States and Canada. Use your computer's search engines to find their bilingual web site.

Leydet Oils
P.O. Box 2354
Fair Oaks, CA 95628

Leydet Oils are sellers of fine essential oils. Their price list can be obtained for $2.00.

The Lucidity Institute
2555 Park Blvd., #2
Palo Alto, CA 94306-1919
E-mail: info@lucidity.com

The Lucidity Institute promotes the study and practice of lucid dreaming. Their catalog carries a wide variety of books, products, and devices that are designed to assist in this art. A quarterly newsletter, called *Nightlight,* is also available. This is another organization that has an extensive web site.

P.O.T.O.
11002 Massachusetts Ave.
Westwood, CA 90025-3510
(310) 575-3717

P.O.T.O. is short for "Procurer Of The Obscure." Their mail-order catalog features services, rare books, and herbs for use by those interested in the magical life. Special orders and requests for the "unusual" are always welcome. You can send $5.00 to receive their current catalog and ordering information.

Soaring Spirit
Valley of the Sun Publishing
P.O. Box 38
Malibu, CA 90265

Valley of the Sun publishes and sells New Age music, mind/body videos, and mind/body audio tapes or CDs, including those designed to aid in astral projection. The first copy of their mag-a-log is free on request, and will continue to be sent to you free of charge for up to a year if you place an order or attend a seminar.

The World Wide Web

If you're on-line, don't rule out the Internet as a great source for learning about and sharing information on any occult art. While gathering information for this book, I requested a search for "astral projection" and came up with 114,169 hits!

Glossary

Akashic Records. An ethereal catalog, accessible through astral projection, containing a detailed historical record of each individual soul (see chapter 11).

alpha. A brain activity level (BAL) associated with the meditative state or light sleep.

altered state of consciousness. A deliberately induced condition in which the normal cycles per second of brain activity is reduced (see chapter 1).

archetype. Symbolic language or image that universally impresses, influences, or directs the human psyche in specific ways (see chapter 9).

aromatherapy. The art of using scent to change a mood, an unwanted condition, or a health concern (see chapter 6).

astral body. The vehicle in which your consciousness travels throughout the astral plane; it can take many forms.

astral classroom. One of the many names for the spiritual learning opportunities afforded on the astral plane. The astral classroom can be both a metaphor and a real classroom setting.

astral plane. An ethereal plane of existence that is conceptualized as being both a parallel to and an interpenetration of our own physical plane; characterized by fluidity of thought, form, and emotion.

astral magic. The art of enacting magical spells while in a state of astral projection.

astral sex. The union of two beings in the astral plane, producing a feeling that is similar to human orgasm.

BAL. An acronym for "Brain Activity Level"; refers to the number of brain waves per second someone produces, thereby defining that person's level of consciousness: beta, alpha, theta, or delta (see chapter 1).

beta. The BAL associated with normal, waking, alert consciousness.

bi-location. The art of being in two places at once—astral and physical—with full consciousness of both of these simultaneous conditions and events.

Body of Light. A vehicle for traveling in the astral plane; also called a Homunculus, a Simulacrum, an Elemental, or a Watcher (see chapter 5).

ceremonial magic. A highly codified magical art based on the Judeo-Christian mystical teaching known as Kaballah and on ancient Egyptian practices.

chakras. The concentrated spheres of energy located within the human body. There are seven primary chakras, and many lesser ones (see chapter 2).

color healing. Using the energy found in the color spectrum to transfer healing energy. This art can be practiced both in the physical and the astral plane (see chapter 12).

collective unconscious. An ethereal repository of thought from the past and future that can be tapped into during meditation or astral projection.

creative visualization. The process of using visualization as a tool for changing one's reality or manifesting one's needs. This is sometimes used in place of, or in conjunction with, forms of natural magic (see chapters 1 and 13).

delta. A BAL associated with very deep sleep or unconsciousness.

divination. The art of foretelling the future based on potentials already put into motion in the present.

doppelgänger. The astral double of a living person; also known as the "fetch" (see chapter 3).

dream control. A dream state in which the dreamer has consciously defined the subject matter and is conscious of the subsequent dream, but is unable to direct the dream action.

elements. The four materials believed by the ancients to comprise the basic structure of all things: earth, water, fire, and air. A fifth element is spirit, which is part of all things but is also separate, and acts as a conduit between physical and non-physical realms.

emotional body. Another name for the astral body.

flying ointment. A magical concoction of herbs and oils whose energies are believed to help assist in astral projection (see chapter 2).

future life progression. The art of gaining impressions or visions of future incarnations.

grounding. The process by which excess energy is harmlessly released from the human body after any magical or occult operation. This is an important final step in any occult exercise and should not be overlooked.

guides. Also called "teachers," these astral beings operate at a very high vibrational rate and watch over or assist a living being during dream time, meditation, or when they are astrally projected.

herbalism. The art of using plant energies to heal or change an unwanted condition.

higher astral. Those parts of the astral plane where beings with higher spiritual vibration rates may dwell or visit.

higher self. An ethereal body, both mental and emotional in nature, that connects the human mind with other intelligences or planes of existence.

human discarnate. A disembodied spirit, or the ghost or soul of someone who once inhabited a living human body.

hypnogogic sleep. The semi-lucid half-sleep state that occurs both on falling asleep and on waking.

karmic. Relating to karma; habits, patterns, unfinished business, or unlearned spiritual lessons carried over from one life to another (as in reincarnation), or from an earlier part of one's current life to a later part.

kiva. The modern definition is an underground ritual chamber. The original Hopi definition refers either to a dwelling or a large room that is set aside for religious purposes.

Land of the Dead. Those regions of the astral plane where the spirits of deceased human or animals dwell.

lift-out. A difficult method of astral projection in which the projector attempts to lift the astral body from the physical one by simply willing it to do so while mentally following along with every step of the transition (see chapter 1).

lower astral. An area of the astral plane where creatures of lower spiritual vibrations live (see chapter 3).

lucid dreaming. A dream state where the dreamer is consciously aware of dreaming and is able to take control of the dream action (see chapter 10).

macrocosm. The entire scope of the universe. Occultists believe it to be reflected in each individual, or in the microcosm.

magic. A confusing term with many levels of meaning. At its most basic, magic is simply the art of controlled transformation, including the art of self-change. Many practitioners of magic believe that desires must be created on the astral plane before they can be made manifest in the physical world (see chapter 13).

mantra. From Sanskrit, originally meaning "a hymn of praise"; a personal chant or phrase used to induce an altered state of consciousness (see chapters 1 and 2).

meditative state. An altered state of consciousness induced with the idea that it will be used for focused thought or spiritual pursuits (see chapter 1).

mysticism. A belief that occult studies and practices can provide a pathway to the realm of the divine or, as it is sometimes called, the Godhead.

natural magic. A magical system based on the belief that all things in nature have energies on which we can draw for assistance in changing realities or attaining needed items or conditions.

OBE. An acronym for "out-of-body experience."

occult. This word has been seen by some as sinister. In truth, it means only "hidden," and is used to refer to a variety of practices and beliefs that once were kept hidden to protect those who practiced them. The term covers a variety of practices that fall outside of the mainstream, including astral projection.

omniscient sight. The phenomenon of viewing things on the astral plane from simultaneous multiple points-of-view, or seeing the full 360-degree spectrum.

pagan. Someone who follows an earth or nature religion, usually one based on pre-Judeo-Christian concepts and divinities. Also called "neo-pagan."

past life regression. The art of gaining impressions or visions of previous incarnations.

progressive relaxation. A meditative process for relaxing the entire body, it teaches you to begin at one individual point (usually the toes or feet) and relax them thoroughly before continuing on up the body (see chapter 1).

prophetic dreams. Dreams that foretell the future.

reincarnation. The belief that the soul returns to inhabit another earthly body after the death of its current physical incarnation.

REM sleep. The "Rapid Eye Movement" sleep characterizing the dream state (see chapter 10).

remote healing. Healing someone from a distance or through astral projection (see chapter 12).

ritual. A prescribed set of actions, gestures, and/or words—often spiritual in content—which rely on symbolic language to steer the mind in a specific direction, and with a specific goal in mind. Rituals may or may not have a religious basis.

shaman. From an archaic Tungus term meaning "between the worlds." A shaman was a tribal priest or priestess who acted as a conduit between the tribe and the deities or otherworld. The shaman was a healer, priest, and fortune teller who used altered states of consciousness to perform tasks.

silver cord. An ethereal connection between the physical body and the astral body in the form of a cord.

Many people believe it roots the traveling astral body with its physical host (see chapter 3)

snap back. A name given to the unpleasant sensation of waking quickly from astral projection; the astral self feels as if it has suddenly collided with the physical self.

soul retrieval. An advanced magical art practiced in many shamanic cultures in which the shaman astrally travels to the spirit world to offer a dying spirit the opportunity to return to the living, or to bring back parts of a soul that may have escaped the physical body due to trauma or illness.

spirit guides. Highly evolved spirit beings whose job it is to assist specific people through life and guide them along their chosen spiritual path.

subconscious mind. The part of the mind that stores information not readily accessible to your conscious mind. This is also the area that governs your astral experiences.

superconscious mind. Like the subconscious, this region stores information not easily retrievable to your consciousness. This is also referred to as the higher mind, higher self, or deep mind; it connects your astral body with other worlds.

tattwa symbols. A set of five geometric symbols that represent the elements: earth, water, fire, air, and spirit. They also function as symbolic gateways to the astral plane (see chapter 9).

theta. A BAL associated with deep meditation and medium-level sleep.

thoughtforms. Images of concentrated thought patterns that manifest and live on the astral plane.

time distortion. The absence of time outside the physical world; it can lead someone to believe that they have spent much more or less time on the astral plane than was estimated.

vedic. Pertaining to the occult and spiritual mysteries of India and south-central Asia.

vibration rate. A spiritual frequency at which all corporeal and astral beings operate. The rate determines the ability of a being to move into the higher astral realms (see chapter 3).

visualization. Mental vision; seeing with your inner eyes, or creating inner world scenarios.

Bibliography

Bibb, Benjamin O. and Joseph J. Weed. *Amazing Secrets of Psychic Healing.* West Nyack, NY: Parker Publishing, 1976.

Bellhayes, Iris. *Spirit Guides.* California: ACS Publications, 1991.

Blackmore, Susan. *Beyond the Body.* Chicago: Academy Chicago Publishers, 1991.

Brennan, J.H. *Astral Doorways.* Wellingborough, Northamptonshire: Aquarian Press, 1986.

———. *Time Travel: A New Perspective.* St. Paul, MN: Llewellyn Worldwide, 1997.

Cockrell, Robert. *The Study and Practice of Astral Projection.* New Hyde Park, NY: University Press, 1966.

Cooper, Jason D. *Esoteric Rune Magic.* St. Paul, MN: Llewellyn Worldwide, 1994.

Conway, D.J. *Astral Love*. St. Paul, MN: Llewellyn Worldwide, 1996.

———. *Flying Without a Broom*. St. Paul, MN: Llewellyn Worldwide, 1995.

Crandall, Joanne. *Self-Transformation Through Music*. Wheaton, IL: The Theosophical Publishing House, 1986.

Cunningham, Scott. *Cunningham's Encyclopedia of Crystal, Gem and Metal Magic*. St. Paul, MN: Llewellyn Worldwide, 1987.

———. *Cunningham's Encyclopedia of Magical Herbs*. St. Paul, MN: Llewellyn Worldwide, 1985.

Denning, Melita and Osborne Phillips. *The Llewellyn Practical Guide to Astral Projection*. St. Paul, MN: Llewellyn Worldwide, 1979.

Eliade, Mircea. *Shamanism: Archaic Techniques of Ecstasy*. Princeton, NJ: The Princeton University Press, 1964.

Galenorn, Yasmine. *Trancing the Witch's Wheel*. St. Paul, MN: Llewellyn Worldwide, 1997.

Greenhouse, Herbert B. *The Astral Journey*. Garden City, NY: Doubleday, 1975.

Grout, Pam. *Jump Start Your Metabolism with the Power of Breath*. Mission, KS: SkillPath Publishing, 1997.

Irwin, Harvey J. *Flight of Mind: A Psychological Study of the Out-Of-Body Experience*. Metuchen, NJ: Scarecrow Press, 1985.

Judith, Anodea. *Wheels of Life: A User's Guide to the Chakra System*. St. Paul, MN: Llewellyn Worldwide, 1987.

Knight, Gareth. *Occult Exercises and Practices*. York Beach, ME: Samuel Weiser, 1976.

LaBerge, Stephen, Ph.D. *Lucid Dreaming*. New York: Ballantine Books, 1986.

Macvey, John W. *Time Travel: A Guide To Journeys In the Fourth Dimension*. Chelsea, MI: Scarborough House, 1990.

McCoy, Edain. *Making Magick: What It Is and How It Works*. St. Paul, MN: Llewellyn Worldwide, 1997.

Mella, Dorothee L. *Stone Power*. New York: Warner Books, 1988.

Miller, Richard Alan. *The Magical and Ritual Use of Herbs*. New York: Destiny Books, 1983.

Monroe, Robert. *Far Journeys*. Garden City, NY: Doubleday, 1985.

———. *Journeys Out-Of-Body*. Garden City, NY: Anchor Press, 1977.

———. *The Ultimate Journey*. New York: Doubleday, 1994.

Muldoon, Sylvan and Hereward Carrington. *The Projection of the Astral Body*. New York: Samuel Weiser, 1970 (originally published 1929).

Ophiel. *The Art and Practice of Astral Projection*. New York: Samuel Weiser, 1961.

Perkins, John. *PsychoNavigation: Techniques for Travel Beyond Time.* Rochester, VT: Destiny Books, 1990.

Rogo, Scott. *Leaving the Body: A Complete Guide to Astral Projection.* Englewood Cliffs, NJ: Prentice-Hall, 1983.

Stack, Rick. *Out-Of-Body Experiences.* Chicago: Contemporary Books, 1988.

Steiger, Brad. *Astral Projection.* West Chester, PA: ParaResearch, 1982.

Stevens, Jose, Ph.D. and Lena S. Stevens. *Secrets of Shamanism: Tapping the Spirit Power Within You.* New York: Avon, 1988.

Taylor, Albert. *Soul Traveler.* Covina, CA: Verity Press, 1996.

Index

Free Catalog

Get the latest information on our body, mind, and spirit products! To receive a **free** copy of Llewellyn's consumer catalog, *New Worlds of Mind & Spirit,* simply call 1-877-NEW-WRLD or visit our website at www.llewellyn.com and click on *New Worlds.*

LLEWELLYN ORDERING INFORMATION

Order Online:
Visit our website at www.llewellyn.com, select your books, and order them on our secure server.

Order by Phone:
- Call toll-free within the U.S. at 1-877-NEW-WRLD (1-877-639-9753). Call toll-free within Canada at 1-866-NEW-WRLD (1-866-639-9753)
- We accept VISA, MasterCard, and American Express

Order by Mail:
Send the full price of your order (MN residents add 6.5% sales tax) in U.S. funds, plus postage & handling to:

Llewellyn Worldwide
2143 Wooddale Drive, Dept. 978-1-56718-625-3
Woodbury, MN 55125-2989

Postage & Handling:
Standard (U.S., Mexico, & Canada). If your order is:
$24.99 and under, add $3.00
$25.00 and over, FREE STANDARD SHIPPING

AK, HI, PR: $15.00 for one book plus $1.00 for each additional book.

International Orders (airmail only):
$16.00 for one book plus $3.00 for each additional book

Orders are processed within 2 business days.
Please allow for normal shipping time. Postage and handling rates subject to change.

Sabbats

Edain McCoy

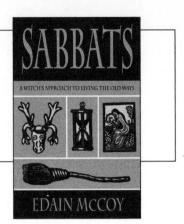

Sabbats offers many fresh, exciting ways to deepen your connection to the turning of the Wheel of the Year. This tremendously practical guide to Pagan solar festivals does more than teach you about the "old ways"—you will learn workable ideas for combining old customs with new expressions of those beliefs that will be congruent with your lifestyle and tradition.

Sabbats begins with background on Paganism (tenets, teachings, and tools) and origins of the eight Sabbats, followed by comprehensive chapters on each Sabbat. These pages are full of ideas for inexpensive seasonal parties in which Pagans and non-Pagans alike can participate, as well as numerous craft ideas and recipes to enrich your celebrations. The last section provides sixteen complete texts of Sabbat rituals—for both covens and solitaries—with detailed guidelines for adapting rituals to specific traditions or individual tastes. Includes an extensive reference section with a resources guide, bibliography, musical scores for rituals, and more.

1-56718-663-7, 7 x 10, 320 pp., illus., photos $18.95

To order, call 1-877-NEW-WRLD
Prices subject to change without notice

Spellworking for Covens

Edain McCoy

Multiply the power! Here's the only book about magick for covens!

While there are numerous books about creating rituals for group use, and others on how to form, organize, and operate covens, this is the first to discuss working magic in a group (of two or more people). Spellworking for Covens addresses raising and sending energy as a group, the power of the group mind, traditional ritual structure, and several types of spells.

To make it even more practical, this book also provides a grimoire containing texts and instructions for actual spells that can be worked within the group setting.

0-7387-0261-7, 7 ½ x 9 ⅛, biblio., index $14.95

To order, call 1-877-NEW-WRLD
Prices subject to change without notice

Advanced Witchcraft

Edain McCoy

Cross the well-guarded threshold into advanced practice with *Advanced Witchcraft*.

The numbers of intermediate practitioners of the Craft are growing. As they stand at the gateway to advanced practice, they need a teacher to guide them on a new and advanced path that will bring them closer to the deities.

Fast-paced, no-nonsense, and thorough, *Advanced Witchcraft* is that teacher. It leaps into the soul of Witchcraft by presuming you've already gone through the beginning and intermediate levels. It challenges your thinking and forces you to gain wisdom through experience. Practical applications include moving into the true realm of shapeshifting, practicing shamanism to heal the shattered soul, pathworking to the source of creation, employing dark witchery without negativity, and much more.

0–7387–0513–6, 336 pp., 7 ½ x 9 ⅛, illus.   **$18.95**

To order, call 1-877-NEW-WRLD
Prices subject to change without notice

Edain McCoy

a practical introduction to the craft

if you want to be a

WITCH

If You Want to be a Witch

Edain McCoy

Choosing the right book to learn about the Old Religion can be quite challenging. *If You Want to Be a Witch* is dedicated to those who want an easy-to-read, yet thorough, introduction to the Craft and its practices.

Filling in the gaps often found in other Wiccan guides, this primer explains the basic tenets of Witchcraft, detailing Wiccan history, philosophy, common traditions, and modern-day ethics. Learn about cyclical time, Wiccan magick and festivals, and how to keep a Book of Shadows. Soon, you'll discover if Witchcraft is the right spiritual path for you and the next steps you can take in the learning process.

0-7387-0514-4, 5 ³⁄₁₆ x 8, 288 pp., illus.   **$12.95**